Hunt for JOY

Hunt & Gather is a spiritual and culinary testimony on the healing powers of whole grains, lean meat, and faith. Dr. Jennifer Hoyt Lalli, a carnivore at heart, shares her passion for venison, and how she reclaimed her health with whole grains. In *Hunt & Gather*, Jennifer guides the reader through a transcendent epicurean journey. It begins with the nutrition of venison, whole grains, and prayer. The first Chapter, for the Carnivores, instructs the reader on how to prepare delectable meals with healthy, tender, non-gamey venison or any lean meat. It includes a tutorial on dressing, preserving, fileting, and cooking to the cut, rather than the recipe. Three modern American-Ethnic fusion dishes are provided for each filet of venison. The following Chapters, save a few pats of butter and eggs, have interestingly resulted in a largely vegan cookbook. The second chapter, for the Grainiacs, details all of the major whole grains and how to prepare them. It includes deliciously innovative recipes that will inspire readers to make whole grains a part of their daily routine. The remaining chapters: for the Breadlers, Omnivores, Frugivores, and Sweet Hearts encourage a well balanced diet. *Hunt & Gather* concludes with Lessons Learned in the Kitchen, Field, and Life to encourage overall well-being, charity, and peace.

Hunt & Gather

Hunt
for JOY

THE HUNT & GATHER PRAYER

If we are what we eat
Then God has bestowed us a noble treat
Venison from the white-tailed deer
So lean, intelligent, strong, and fair

We respect this Heavenly herbivore
Who humbles us earthly carnivores
Because of your power, wit, and stealth
You instill in us ~ patience, hope, and health

With your Majestic Crown and Magnificent Meat
We Honor You through Prayer and Plate
Thanks to God's Plan and Our Fate
We Break Bread Now – *Always* – and Celebrate

~ Amen

This Book Recounts how Venison
and Whole Grains Saved My Body & Soul

At Age 39, I have more Energy and Faith than Ever
My Prayer is that You Share in this Feeling

I Seek Venison in my Pursuit of *Happiness*
I Rely on Whole Grains for the Pursuit of *Healthfulness*

For Carnivores, Grainiacs, Vegans, & Vegetarians who
Hunt, Gather, Forage, Harvest & Love

And God blessed Noah and his sons, and said...

Every moving thing that liveth shall be meat for you; even as the green herb have I given you all things.

~ Genesis 9:1, 9:3 KJV

Hunt & Gather

The Healing Powers of Whole Grains, Lean Meat, and Prayer

Jennifer Hoyt Lalli

PHOTOGRAPHY: JENNIFER LALLI

www.huntforjoy.com

Mill City Press, Inc.
2301 Lucien Way #415
Maitland, FL 32751
407.339.4217
www.millcitypress.net

Library of Congress Cataloging-in-Publication Data is available upon request
Lalli, Jennifer
Hunt & gather: the healing powers of whole grains, lean meat, and prayer / by Jennifer Lalli;
photographs by Jennifer Lalli; preface by Pastor Shake Smith, contribution by Chris Lalli.
Includes bibliographical references and index by Jennifer Lalli.

First Edition ISBN: 978-0-9911-6950-4
1. Cooking, Religion

Second Edition - 2021
Paperback ISBN-13: 978-1-6628-3844-6
Hard Cover ISBN-13: 978-1-6628-3845-3
Ebook ISBN-13: 978-1-6628-3846-0

This Book is dedicated to Chris, Tristan, and Milla
& Healing Others through God's Grace and Nutrition

For with God
nothing shall be impossible
- Luke 1:37 KJV

If *it* is God's Will, *it* will *be*

~ J. H. Lalli

In Loving Memory of Alexandra and Barlow Lalli, Annie Krull,
Kimberly Staub, Grandma & Grandpa Hoyt, Grandma & Grandpa
Guillory who are now Eternally with our Father

Contents

Table of Contents

Abbreviations, Conversions & How to Use this Book

Tbs: Tablespoon: big T, big spoon   tsp: teaspoon: little t, little spoon

lb: pound, or lbs, for pounds   oz: ounce or ounce

g: gram or grams   gal: gallon

kg: kilogram   qt: quart

3 tsp ≈ 1 Tbs   2 oz ≈ 4 Tbs ≈ ¼ cup

2 Tbs ≈ ⅛ cup   8 oz ≈ 1 cup

4 Tbs ≈ ¼ cup: remember the 4s   2 cups ≈ 1 pint

1 cup ≈ 16 Tbs   4 cups ≈ 1 quart

⅓ cup ≈ 5 ⅓ Tbs, or, 5 Tbs + 1 tsp   4 quarts ≈ 1 gallon

28.4 g ≈ 1 oz ≈ 2 Tbs ≈ ⅛ cup   16 oz ≈ 1 lb

i.e.   for example

≈   roughly equals (i.e., weight equivalents are rough as food densities vary)

~   about (for weight or time of mixing, kneading, or cooking)

temp   temperature

med   medium (as in heat or mixing speed with an electric mixer)

hr   hour or hours

min   minute or minutes

sec   second or seconds

Tips:

- time: set a timer for best results
- garlic: recipes herein use large cloves; 2 small = 1 large; peel and trim root ends; use suggested sauté times to avoid bitterness as minced garlic can burn quickly
- butter: all recipes herein use unsalted butter
- soften butter: microwave it in ~ 10 sec intervals on a plate to desired consistency
- salt: use fine grain when baking for even distribution and to pass through a sifter
- eggs: choose extra large or large, organic, cage-free when possible
- wine: cook with wine you would drink; deglazing cooks most of the alcohol off

Bibles:

KJV: King James Version   NCV: New Century Version

NKJV: New King James Version   NIV: New International Version

Venison and Hunting: You do not *need* venison for this book

- Any lean red meat or pork, commercial or wild, can be substituted for the venison
- You do not need to hunt to eat venison; purchase it, or barter with friends
- If you are a hunter, but do not eat venison; donate it, see Resources (page 266)

Health:

- I am not an M.D. Follow a trusted doctor's advice before entering into any diet

Serving Size:

- Not included without knowing appetites or planned meal course, estimates follow:
  - Carnivores & Vegetables: 2 – 4; Grain & Bean Salads: 4 – 12; Soups: 4 - 8

Cooking Techniques & Specialty Foods:

- Techniques and tips are given in Lessons Learned in the Kitchen (page 253)
- Notes on specialty foods are given in Pantry and Resources (page 262 and 266)

Oven Modes & Oven Temperature:

- Oven temperatures are given in degrees Fahrenheit (°F)
- Oven (modes) are given after temp as: Details: Preheat oven to 380 °F (roast)
- Common modes include: bake, roast, broil, bake stone, convection, convection bake, convection roast, convection broil, convection dehydration, and proof
- The location of the oven's heat source is what differentiates each mode:
  - Bake: heat source from bottom – to cook pie crusts, cakes, or cookies
  - Roast: heat source from top – for browning meat or toasting
  - Broil: intense from top – to sear meat, melt cheese, or caramelize sugar
  - Convection: fans circulate air movement for uniform cooking – to promote even baking or dehydrating on several racks, to roast tender cuts of meat, to broil thick cuts of meat, or to yield crispy potatoes, vegetables and pies
  - Proof: very low temperature (80 – 110 °F) – to proof or rise bread dough

Recommended Oven Rack Positions:

- Roasting - upper third of the oven to brown meat
- Baking - lower third to promote cooking on the bottom
- Broiling - top rack, a few inches below the intense direct heat source
- Unsure - use the middle rack to prevent over browning the top or bottom

Introduction

Preface

It is an honor for me to be asked by Jen to write the preface for this cookbook. As you will quickly learn, it is much more than your average cookbook with ordinary recipes. In the following pages, you will see her genuine love for God and her husband, and her desire for delicious, healthy cooking. My wife and I have had the privilege to enjoy several meals prepared by Jen in her kitchen.

You will also quickly learn that Chris and Jen have a love for God's creation and spending time together in the great outdoors. That's how we connected when they first came to church. As a fellow outdoorsman, many of my sermons deal with hunting and fishing. Growing up, my mom regularly prepared meals with rabbit, squirrel, quail, turkey or deer that we had taken.

Enjoy each section of Jen's project. Her heart and soul have been poured into it. Learn the importance of good nutrition. The information she is sharing on preparing venison and her overall knowledge of cooking is incredible.

Most importantly, enjoy the scripture verses that are shared from God's Word. She carefully selected these as she prayed and asked the Lord for His guidance in her writing. This book may be used to be feed both physically and spiritually.

When I first met Chris and Jen, I had the privilege to share God's love with them, see them accept Jesus Christ as their personal Savior and baptize them. We are so blessed to have them as a part of our church family. If you do not know Christ and have a personal relationship with Him, please take time to receive the gift of salvation found in Him.

"For God so loved the world, that He gave His only begotten Son, that whosoever believeth in Him should not perish, but have everlasting life."
— John 3:16 KJV

Shake Smith, Pastor
Auburn Baptist Church
Riner, Virginia

My Treestand is my Chapel

The Lord God is my strength.
He makes me like a deer that does not stumble so I can walk on
the steep mountains.

~ Habakkuk 3:19 NCV

When I first started hunting, I didn't know what to do with my time - alone, for hours, way up high in the trees, alone.

I would photograph squirrels, gawk at the sunrise and sunset, eat Sweet Tarts, text, and think about bears and my escape plan. After my first hunt, I immediately realized that it was the most quiet and serene event I had experienced in years, or possibly ever. Like you, I lead a stressful life. My time in the stand is my escape, and I can now appreciate why people get hooked on hunting. It is not the hunt, but rather the entire experience. To me, nothing says Fall like the smell of "scent-free" spray. I love it. I love the gear. I love my Hoyt® bow and my coincidental maiden name. I love the satisfaction of a great arrow grouping. I love walking outside in the dark to gaze at the same starry sky only the forest knows. I love being in a tree before the birds sing or the moon has set. I love losing a few pounds over the weekend after hiking miles to hang treestands, and gaining them right back after one phenomenal meal. I love the small victories of surviving the cold. I love being a part of something that Chris, my husband, loves. I love learning from him and making him laugh. I love being self-reliant, thanks to God's land. Above all, I love my time with God. **I am never alone.**

For Saturday hunts, we'd sit for 4 - 12 hours at a time in the stands. After work, I'd sit in the blind for at least an hour or two. This is when I started reading Watchman Nee. I then moved on to the Bible. It changed my life. I stopped texting and started praying.

I realize that I am blessed because of all of the prayers that my family and friends have sent to God for me. Now it is time to give it all back. **My Treestand is my Chapel.**

Pray continually, and give thanks whatever happens.
That is what God wants for you in Christ Jesus.
~ 1 Thessalonians 5:17-18 NCV

My brethren, count it all joy when you fall into various trials, knowing that the testing of your faith produces patience.
~ James 1:2-3 NKJV

Pride will ruin people, but those who are humble will be honored.
~ Proverbs 29:23 NCV

Healthy Body

About the Author, Becoming a Grainiac

This book is my culinary and spiritual testimony as to how whole grains healed my body and how hunting saved my soul. What follows is the story of a girl who was born a carnivore, became a chemist, evolved into a grainiac and omnivore; and was born again.

I used to be a serious **carnivore**. Born in 1974 to Rosemary and Joseph Hoyt in Wilkes-Barre, PA, I recall eating an egg sandwich for breakfast, a roast beef sandwich (without the bread) for lunch, and meat for dinner - every day. My Mom recalls that, as an infant, I stopped eating fruits and vegetables once I was old enough to eat pureed meat. If I didn't eat meat, I did not feel as though I had eaten anything. In my twenties, I met my future husband Chris at Virginia Tech. I cooked dinner for him one evening when we started dating. He told me how great everything looked and cautiously asked, "Are we having anything else with the steak?" I said, "Yes, I could make you another if you'd like". He was thrilled until he realized I wasn't kidding.

Recently, I made a beautiful prime rib with roasted vegetables for my Dad and his friends; but he barely touched the meat. I asked him when he had started cutting back on meat, since we ate steak almost every day of my childhood. He said, "That was *your* favorite food, so we made it for you". Talk about sacrifice. Thanks Dad!

A **grainiac** is someone who has a healthy obsession with whole grains. Not only do I love them; I literally cannot function without them. I began having health problems about ten years ago that became serious. I was on my way to permanent, life-altering surgery. As a last resort, my husband suggested I seek counsel from a certified dietician; and my doctor concurred. The dietician recommended a macrobiotics-based diet centered on gluten-free grains to rule out celiac disease (see page 107). It turned out that whole grains, with or without gluten, was exactly what I was missing. By replacing refined and processed foods with whole grains, fruit, and lean meat, my body began to heal itself. Over the next few years, I stuck with this new diet, avoided surgery, and reclaimed my health. Additionally, my energy level, spirit, and joy have been seemingly limitless since.

Peaceful Soul

On our Hunt for Deer, we Found God

As I sit by the window chewing slowly on each grain of my spelt salad, I ponder my past and thank God for the present. I thank God for the cat purring peacefully on my lap and for the skills of our Veterinarian who gave our other cat one more of her 9 lives. I am in awe of the birds bathing and chipmunks playing, as the bright sun rises before us. I daydream about recipes that we will enjoy, and perhaps help others, and how to make today the best day ever. This is not how I used to start my day, or who I used to be. While things may make you happy, **peace through God's grace brings joy**.

On our hunt for deer, we found God. My husband Chris, a hunter, fly fisher, and fly-tying phenom, has hunted since the first day he was legally allowed. A few years ago, he wanted to expand his hunting season and challenge himself through bow hunting. He bought his first compound bow and became fast friends with our local shop's resident bow expert, Chris Ramrattan. Chris and his wife Jess changed our lives by introducing us to Auburn Baptist Church (ABC) in Riner, VA. We were hoping to become better archers, and they were praying we would find God. We loved ABC after our first visit, but we didn't know how much we would need it in the years to come.

I have always been a happy and positive person. Through my family's love and guidance, I have also known that most anything is possible with hard work, luck, and determination. What I didn't know was, that with God, miracles are possible too. I used to dwell on everything and let stress control me. After joining ABC, I have finally come to know what peace, joy, and love are. Chris and I were baptized in the Little River,  in Floyd County, VA by Pastor Stanley "Shake" Smith, in front of hundreds of members who supported us. It was Pastor Shake who introduced us to the concept of JOY (Jesus, Others, You). Shake is an avid hunter and outdoorsman who loves God's Church, America, milk shakes, and Christ. Everyone who knows him is thankful they do.

Venison Nutrition

Wild animals are active. Farm-raised animals graze. Think about this the next time you exercise and how full time athletes may look in comparison.

Lean – Venison has < 1 g of fat / oz. For comparison: lean beef has ~ 2 g fat / oz, and marbled beef contains 6 - 9 g fat / oz. Less than ⅓ of venison's fat is saturated fat, relative to ½ of beef's fat. Beef also contains more than three times the cholesterol of venison. For example, a 4 oz cut porterhouse steak contains 76 mg, where as a 4 oz cut of venison has 20 mg. The recommended daily intake for cholesterol is < 300 mg. You can, and should still enjoy beef, but like anything else in life, in moderation.

Green – Wild venison is naturally free of hormones, steroids, and antibiotics. Beyond the gas in your car, little crude oil is needed to bring wild game to your table. For cattle, grass-fed require much less fuel than feedstock raised (~70 verses 250 gal/lifetime).

Light – While both beef and venison contain zero carbohydrates, venison is naturally lower in calories due to its lower fat content. Average calories within 4 oz servings of meat are: venison (125), sirloin beef (240), and porterhouse beef (310).

Powerful – Venison is rich in iron, protein, minerals, and B-vitamins (1, 2, 3, 5, 6, and 12).

Venison offers ~ 3.3 mg iron / 4 oz portion, which is roughly ⅓ more than sirloin. Adults should consume ~9 ~ 18 mg of iron daily, as it is helpful in preventing anemia, transporting oxygen throughout the body, and creating connective tissue.

Venison and beef each contain ~ 25 g protein / 4 oz serving, and are considered "complete proteins", as each contain all 10 of our essential amino acids. Amino acids are responsible for our body's chemical reactions and play a role in metabolic function.

The U.S., Food and Drug Administration (FDA) also cites venison as an excellent source of: niacin (B-3), riboflavin (B-6) and thiamin (B-12); providing 37 %, 24 % and 15% of our respective required daily amount. Vitamin B is vital to our metabolic and cardiovascular health, and necessary for a properly functioning nervous system. Venison is additionally a source of: folate, vitamin D, vitamin E, phosphorus, selenium, copper, zinc, magnesium, manganese, potassium, and omega-3 fatty acids.

Whole Grain Nutrition

Whole grains offer 100% of the bran, germ and endosperm. Refined grains are processed. Think about what might be missing next time you opt for white over wheat.

A Form of Inexpensive Health Insurance – is available for those who want it and are willing to work for it. Whole grains are absurdly **inexpensive**, pennies per pound for most, but you have to know how to cook them, and make them taste good. If you don't like it, you won't eat it or much less cook it. In numerous studies, whole grains have repeatedly demonstrated average risk reductions of strokes by 33%, heart disease by 27%, and type 2 diabetes by 26%. Additional studies verify that whole grains reduce your risk for cancer, obesity, asthma, and inflammatory diseases, while improving the health of your carotid arteries and blood pressure. The medicinal power of whole grains is attributed to their powerhouse package of soluble and insoluble fiber, healthy fats, vitamins, minerals, plant enzymes, hormones, and hundreds of phytochemicals.

Digestive Health – of Americans is poor. According to the 2013 statistics from the Cancer Institute at the National Institutes of Health, colorectal cancer is the second deadliest type (with 50,830 fatalities) after lung (with 159,480), and preceding breast (with 40,030). As of April 2013, estimated new cases for colorectal cancer in the U.S. are 142,820. Sobering data from 2007 - 2009, suggest that 1 out of every 20 Americans born today, will be diagnosed with colorectal cancer at some period during their lifetime. Encouraging news is that screening, diet, and exercise can reduce this threat. The American Cancer Society cites large recent studies substantiating that fiber intake, especially from whole grains, may lower the risk of colorectal cancer.

Low Fat & High Fiber – may be the answer. It is known that soluble fiber lowers cholesterol and insoluble fiber moves waste through the digestive tract. It was Dr. Denis Burkitt's pioneering research on whole grains that led to our current awareness of the health benefits of fiber. During his tour as an Army physician in World War II, and as President of the Christian Medical Fellowship, he spent many years in Kenya, Somalia, and Uganda. He found a striking absence of bowel diseases in native Africans who consumed high fiber diets (millet, teff, corn, and brown rice) relative to a high incidence of such diseases in his fellow Brits who consumed low fiber refined carbohydrates. He concluded that many Western diseases were the result of diet and lifestyle.

The Nutrition of Prayer

In a time of physical and spiritual need, I read several books that changed my life. They include: Cary Schmidt's *Done*, C.S. Lewis's *The Screwtape Letters*, Watchman Nee's *New Believer's Series*, and God's *Holy Bible*. These books were my ultimate nutrition.

Today, it is widely accepted that reducing stress leads to overall improvements in health and recovery from seemingly unmanageable ailments. The body needs food to survive. The body and soul both benefit from prayer. The power of prayer is undeniable.

Done - If you can accept God's grace, and trust Him with your eternal soul, how can you not trust him with the small things in your daily life here on Earth? Think about this.

The Screwtape Letters - Worry is the single most effective weapon against enjoying today. When you stop worrying, and start living, you may come to realize that Heaven is not a place you are going, it is where we are living - right now.

New Believer Series – People plan, God laughs. Understanding prayer, Church, Christianity, humanity, judgment, and forgiveness are all key to leading a peaceful life. When you can finally accept God's plan and truly "let go, and let God" prayer will take on new meaning. Understanding that your requests might not fit God's plan may be the single most effective thing you can do to reduce stress in your life.

The Bible - My problems are no worse than yours, so I won't bore you with my details. After reading Matthew, we asked, and we received; but in many cases, it was not for what we asked. Rather, our hearts were broken again and again. Once we opened our souls to God's gifts, rather than our requests, we started witnessing miracles. How could we possibly ask for anything more?

While the Bible is continually being pushed out of our daily lives, I pray that the tidbits of scripture herein might inspire you to reach for it to get the whole story. It truly contains all of the answers and recipes for a healthy soul. God Bless You and Yours.

And he humbled thee, and suffered thee to hunger, and fed thee with man'-na, which thou knewest not, neither did thy fathers know; that he might make thee know that man doth not live by bread only, but by every word that proceedeth out of the mouth of the Lord doth man live.

– Old Testament, Deuteronomy 8:3 KJV

If we will not learn to eat the only food that the universe grows – the only food that any possible universe can ever grow – then we must starve eternally.

– C.S. Lewis on the Bible

It is written that man shall not live on bread alone, but by every word that proceedeth out of the mouth of God.

~ New Testament, Matthew 4:4 KJV

Methods and Equipment
About the Book ~ Becoming a Venison Cook

VENISON

Each of the venison recipes herein was developed to yield tender, "non-gamey", modern American-Ethnic fusions, and can all be used with your favorite wild game (buffalo, elk, caribou) or farm raised (cow, lamb, pork) meat. Many of the cuts are interchangeable. A good knife, cutting board, ovenproof pan, and oven mitts are all you need to start. Follow the recipes, or experiment; you may learn either way.

KEEP IT SIMPLE, then EXPERIMENT

So simple, yet so good... That is how you should feel about venison once you start cooking with properly processed meat. You can get started with this book immediately with store bought meat, perfect cuts of venison from your local butcher, or with wild game from your freezer.

Once we started processing our own venison, we have yet to taste anything "gamey". Your butcher can provide you with the same or even better results. The key is to cool the meat immediately and quickly in the field, remove all of the blood, and freeze clean cuts in airtight bags. If you don't hack through the bones creating shards, or freeze filets of meat in unlined tin foil, in other words - treat your game with the same respect you would store bought meat - you will be successful.

Mature bucks are typically less tender than young does. If you are concerned about toughness, use a recipe that includes wine, a marinade, the crock-pot, or a sauce. You'll be surprised at how well you can honor your trophy buck on the wall a second time on the table. While bacon is delicious, you don't need it for every game recipe.

If you are new to venison, I would recommend starting with the simple recipes, such as The Easiest Dinner Ever (flavorful), Tender Loins (tender), or Bordeaux Backstraps (exquisite taste and melt-in-your mouth texture). These recipes demonstrate how easy it is to bring delicious dethawed game from the field to your table in less than 20 minutes. These dishes may rival the best steak you have ever had, with nearly 0% fat.

Work your way through the recipes with increasing complexity and ingredients as you familiarize yourself with the taste of wild game. Start with an astoundingly easy crock-pot recipe such as Fall-Apart Venison Goulash. Next, try one of the kabob recipes, (Smoky Chipotle, or Broiled Jalapeño) which require a simple marinade followed by a brief sear on the grill or under the broiler.

If you are adept in the kitchen, dive right in and start with any recipe in the book. If you are new to cooking and want to try something that looks challenging (but isn't), try the Venison Loin Black Bean Chili Verde, 17 Pepper Venison Chili, or Venison Bolognese. These are my favorite recipes because they took so many iterations to get the ratios just right. They also use my bowl or batch method of cooking. When a recipe includes a lot of ingredients, I separate them into batches of two or three bowls to make the dish seem less intimidating. This keeps me on track so that each batch of ingredients is ready to be added at the right stage in the process. You will prevent scorching foods this way mid-sauté.

HOW DO I COOK THIS?

When we give venison to our friends, their first question is often:

"How do I cook this?"

The answer:

"The same way you would a lean piece of red meat."

The three key items to cooking with venison are:
1. Know the type of cut (filet) with which you are working – cook to your cut
2. Do not overcook – over-heating dries, and over-marinating cures/cooks
3. For mature bucks or tough cuts - grind the meat, or use a crock pot or sauce

The biggest misconception about venison is that you have to "do something special" to remove the gaminess, such as, wrap it with fat, or break down the toughness with acid. I used to cook our venison at very low temperatures for extended periods of time in the oven because I heard that is what was needed. This just dries the meat out, akin to making beef jerky, but thick and inedible. I finally stopped following directions and watched my husband treat the meat like beef by throwing it on the grill. It worked. Once I had success with backstraps and tenderloins, I then moved on to the other cuts and guessed at what preparation might work best. I have made variations on every recipe in this book and finally decided to start documenting things that worked and tasted great. I offer these recipes to you with encouragement to modify them.

Learn what the different cuts of beef are on your next stroll through the supermarket and practice with these. Since beef has a higher fat content, you could trim it to mimic venison. To gain confidence, I would recommend investing in a meat thermometer for < $10 to verify the "doneness" in the thickest portion. Until you get the feel of cooking based on the size and thickness, for all recipes herein, measure the temperature in the thickest portion, press on it, or cut the meat in the center to view the color per the following guidelines:

- Rare: 120-125 °F – cool bright red center, soft
- Medium-Rare: 130 °F – warm red center, less soft
- Medium: 140 °F – pink, semi-firm
- Medium-Well: 150 °F – thick gray-brown edges and pink center, firm
- Well Done: 160 °F – gray-brown throughout entire thickness, tough

VENISON RETRIEVING & PROCESSING

You will need a gutting knife to remove the innards in the field. Then, cut a small hole in the back of each hind leg at the Achilles. Push a 3' long branch into the holes and use it as a handle to drag your deer out of the woods quickly to its next destination. If you are processing the meat yourself, a tripod or hitch hoist (~$149) will prove indispensable. A stainless or polyethylene table ($49 ~ $79), sharp knife, plenty of paper towels, and a bucket of water will simplify the filleting task.

VENISON GRINDING

For grinding, a meat grinder (starting at $24), will allow you to control the fat within your ground venison to produce customized jerky, Bolognese sauce, taco, burger, or sausage blends with 0 – 20% fat. A mixer attachment (~$49) works just as well as a stand-alone grinder (~$70 - $200) for small jobs. Be sure to wash the metal parts after grinding with soap and water, and dry thoroughly to prevent rusting.

VENISON STORAGE & PRESERVATION

For storage, nothing beats a vacuum-sealed bag. This is one of the keys to fresh tasting, tender game. You can purchase a Ziploc® Vacuum Starter Kit at the grocery store for ~$5. If you plan to seal frequently, you might consider an electric vacuum sealer (~$70 – 200), which utilizes rolls of vacuum sealing plastic that minimizes waste. They are easy to use and keep meat fresh for over a year. Label each bag using a Sharpie with the date, type of deer (doe or buck), age (mature or young), and the cut. This will allow you to choose the right recipe without question.

DEHYDRATING VENISON JERKY

You do not need a dehydrator to make great jerky; nor do you need a meat grinder. My oven worked great on the first attempt. I do not currently own a dehydrator, but am stalking several models by TSM, Sedona, Excalibur®, and Cabela's®.

WHOLE GRAINS, LEGUMES, & PRESSURE COOKING

Each of the whole grain recipes herein can be prepared with boiling water in a saucepan; although, the modern, safe, electric pressure cooker has changed my life. An investment of roughly $99 may save you a life of pain and doctor bills as it has for me. Whole grains and dried beans are cooked in minutes, not hours. Guesswork on done-ness and pre-soaking are virtually eliminated with a pressure cooker.

STORING WHOLE GRAINS

Whole grains, with their oil-rich germ intact, are living foods that should be stored in airtight containers and out of direct sunlight. My favorite containers are: Bob's Red Mill® bags with their free red closures provided with online orders, 9" x 6" Silver Zip Lock Stand-Up Pouches (25 for ~$8), and Oxo POP containers (~$10 each). For fun, a label maker ($20) will keep you organized and your friends amused.

WHOLE WHEAT FLOUR & MILLING

None of the recipes herein require a grain mill, although I prefer grinding my grains to allow for unlimited flour varieties, unsurpassed freshness, maximum nutrient content, and mere enjoyment. Grain mills start at ~$49. Because whole grain flours are also living, they should ideally be refrigerated. With a mill, you will save money and refrigerator space by grinding only what you need, rather than wasting rancid flour.

JUICING

The included juice recipes work with a high-speed (~$99) or low-speed, masticating juicer (~$369). Smoothies work best with a high-speed blender ($49) or super-high speed Vitamix® (~$375). Juicing is fun, but can get expensive; though it allows for an extraordinarily high intake of vitamins and minerals due to the dense blends of fruits or vegetables that most individuals would not normally consume in any one sitting.

Szechuan, Tellicherry, White, Pink, and Green Peppercorns with Sea Salt

NEED vs. WANT

NEED - $97.80 (see Resources, page 266)

To get started, you will need: a Chef's knife, sharpening hone, and cutting board. I reach for my 10" Wüsthof knife 99% of the time. You only need one, but it needs to feel good in your hands. Knife prices vary widely, from tens to upwards of thousands of dollars. For cutting boards, I love Epicurean® wood composites with rubber feet, which prevent slipping, and scratching your countertops. **Sea salt and peppercorns** are the two most important ingredients in any recipe. Invest in a good pepper mill and cute salt cellar. For $97.80, here are a few items with excellent reviews to get you started:

- $29.95 – Victorinox 8" Chef's knife
- $24.95 – Epicurean Non-Slip Cutting Board
- $19.95 – Wüsthof sharpening steel
- $22.95 – Peugeot Nancy Adjustable Grind Pepper or Salt Mill

WANT - $88.79 (see Resources, page 266)

Below are items I use nearly every day. You may want to add these to your wish list.

- $24.95 – Chef'n® Fresh Force™ Citrus Juicer: Fresh citrus juice heightens the flavor of so many dishes and transforms water into a health drink. This little juicer keeps my hands clean, prevents acidic burns, and catches all of the seeds.
- $14.95 - Microplane® Cut Resistant Glove: I wear this when grating food or deseeding peppers. It prevents capsaicin burns (see page 253) and incisions.
- $12.95 – Waffle Weave Microfiber Towels from Williams-Sonoma: These are the most absorbent, softest, lint free towels I have ever used. I dry my hands and clean with them constantly.
- $29.95 – Melamine Bowls, Set of 3 from Williams-Sonoma: These handled bowls are cute, lightweight, do not slip, keep me organized, and survive most everything.
- $5.99 – Taylor® Digital Timer: You could certainly rely on a clock while cooking, but who couldn't benefit from the reminder of a chime when multi-tasking.

HAVE FUN - Don't be Penny-wise Pound-foolish. Specialized kitchen appliances encourage cooking, good health, and fun. You may rationalize hunting by claiming the cost savings of not buying beef. Don't kid yourself. Beef is good! Don't stop eating it. Hunting and cooking can be expensive hobbies, but they don't need to be. No matter the equipment, you can't put a price on time with God, Family, Friends, and Nature.

Thermal Conductivity of Cookware

Material	Mass density ρ = g/cc	Thermal Conductivity κ = W/m·K	Specific Heat per cubic centimeter C/cc = J/(cc·K)
Diamond	3.3	~ 2000	
Silver (Ag)	10.5	429	
Copper (Cu)	8.9	401	3.44
Gold (Au)	19.3	318	
Aluminum (Al)	2.7	237	2.42
Iron (Fe)	7.9	80	3.53
Cast Iron (≥ 2.1% C)	7.3	55	3.78
Carbon Steel (0.12 – 2.0% C)	7.8	51	
Stainless Steel (≥ 10.5% Cr)	7.7	18	3.95
Ceramic	1.9	1.5	
Glass (Si)	2.5	0.8	
Nonstick (polymer)	1.2	0.2	
Water	1.0	0.6	
Air	0.001	0.02	

Thermal Conductivity (κ) – of cookware is the rate at which it can conduct heat from one area to another. It is measured in watts per meter per degree Kelvin (W/m·K). Materials with high κ respond rapidly to heat source changes and offer enhanced evenness, thus fewer hot spots, and less burnt food. Diamond has the highest κ of any material, though it is much too hard and expensive for cookware. Royalty used to cook with Ag, though it is too soft and reactive for realistic use. While Cu's κ (401) is roughly double that of Al (237), its weight and cost are approximately three times more.

Reactivity – stainless steel, enameled cast iron, anodized aluminum, and new nonstick polymers are non-reactive and food safe. Copper, aluminum, iron, and carbon steel each require seasoning or a topcoat to prevent reactions with food or rusting.

Heat Capacity (C) – of cookware is the amount of heat it can retain. A material's specific, C, is given in Joules per gram per degree Kelvin (J/g·K). Interestingly, Al has a C of 0.897 which is double that of 0.449 for Fe. Although, since Al's density is roughly ⅓ that of Fe, you would need an Al pan ~ 3x as thick as your cast iron pan to match its renown heat retention properties. When C is multiplied by density, C/cc results in 3.78 for cast iron and 2.42 for Al. Cast iron can keep food warm without the flame, though it could also burn a custard or sauce as it has poor responsiveness. Ideally, the pan must be able to continuously transfer its heat to the food, rather than vice versa.

Husband of the Year, Chris Lalli: 2002 – present
Lifetime Achievement Award Earned in 2009

Half way through grad school, I started cooking (mostly steak of course) on an electric range with All-Clad 18/10 Stainless cookware. This high quality steel is an iron alloy that contains 18% nickel (Ni) and 10% chromium (Cr). It prevents corrosion and rusting, which can occur with cast iron or carbon steel if improperly seasoned. As a polymer chemist, I initially considered nonstick cookware. Though, my dissertation was focused on thermally conductive adhesives, so I dreamed of someday cooking with copper on a gas range. Ten years later, my dream came true and Chris won his prestigious award.

In designing our kitchen, I wanted two people to be able to cook at once on a range top and at an island; although gas burners require ventilation hoods per code. Since I was fixated on hanging a chandelier above the island, I resolved to set up a "grease station" at the range and a "water only" area on the island. This would allow one person to sear and splatter under the hood, while the other boiled grains or made meringues. For the island, we could then choose between an induction or electric cooktop. I was intrigued by induction based on the claims of speed and precision. One issue was that copper is not compatible, as induction cooktops require cookware with a magnetic component.

An experiment had to be conducted. Not telling Chris my plan, I asked him to give up a Saturday to help me carry an unwieldy box of cookware (3 copper, 3 stainless, and 3 enameled cast iron pots) into a kitchen appliance store. I "needed" 3 of each so that no heat source had the unfair advantage of a preheated pot. Armed with a measuring cup and timer, I boiled water on their gas range, induction, and electric heat sources. Chris was such a good sport. He was equally embarrassed and entertained watching customers laughing at me. All business, I verified induction as the clear victor.

If I could own only one pan, it would be my Mauviel Copper 3.2 qt Sauté with a lid, stainless liner, and handle. It is ovenproof for roasting, and can deglaze sauces over a flame, whereas a ceramic casserole cannot. If I could have two pieces, I would add a 3.6 qt covered saucepan (copper or stainless steel for induction) for cooking grains, and with a  rolled edge for pouring soups. Finally, I would invest in an 8 or 10 qt Dutch oven (enameled cast iron, copper, or stainless steel) for chilies, stews, and pasta.

Bows, Crossbows, Muzzleloaders, and Rifles
Maximize your Hunting Season – a Patient Heart makes it Fun

First day hunting with Husband, Chris Lalli, and my First Bow

First hunt with Dad, Joseph Hoyt, and his Personalized Crossbow

Now therefore, please take your weapons, your quiver, and your bow, and go out to the field and hunt game for me.

~ Genesis 27:3 NKJV

I shot my first compound bow, an awesome little pink PSE, at age 34. Amused by my coincidental maiden name, I then 'Got Serious, and Got Hoyt' and started bow hunting with a camouflage Hoyt bow at 35. I became a Christian at 36, and finally allowed my husband to teach me how to hunt with firearms at 37. We convinced my Dad, at age 61, to try crossbow hunting in late 2012. Now, we all go every chance we get. It is never too late to learn something new, spend more time with family, or accept Jesus Christ's will in your life. Teaching and learning can be the ultimate tests of patience, kindness, and trust. I am 39 today, and have never had more energy, faith, or joy knowing that the future holds what God has in mind; and He is always good.

Patience and encouragement come from God.

~ Romans 15:5 NCV

Love is patient and kind. Love is not jealous, it does not brag, and it is not proud. Love is not rude, is not selfish, and does not get upset with others. Love does not count up wrongs that have been done. Love is not happy with evil but is happy with the truth. Love patiently accepts all things. It always trusts, always hopes, and always remains strong.
Love never ends.

~ 1 Corinthians 13:4-8 NCV

These are the beasts which ye shall eat: the ox, the sheep, and the goat, the hart, and the roebuck, and **the fallow deer**, and the wild goat, and the pygarg, and the wild ox, and the chamois.   ~ Deuteronomy 14:4-6 KJV

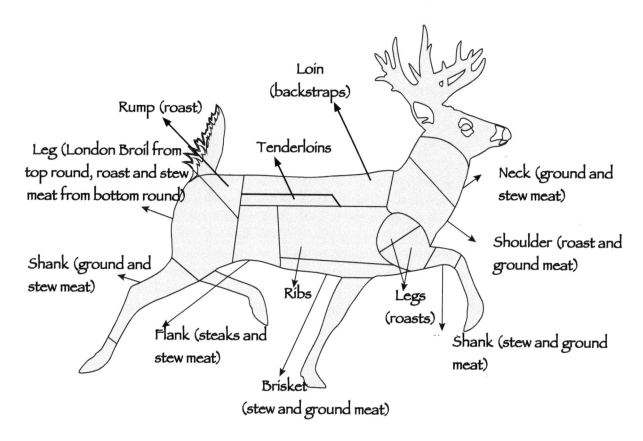

In Vienna, Austria, restaurateurs encourage their diners to order a specific cut of beef, rather than just the menu item. We experienced this first hand at two of the world-famous Plachutta Restaurants, renowned for their Tafelspitz, a classic Viennese prime boiled beef dish. Their menu depicts a sketch of the cow; and their hosts review the characteristics of each filet. Guests appreciate the great pride they take in their quality beef source, as their farmers can trace each animal back to its birth. At Plachutta, Tafelspitz is brought to the table in copper pots, dogs are welcome to join their owners for dinner under the table, and patrons are treated like royalty. In this chapter, I encourage you to do the same by focusing on the venison filet, rather than the recipe; and honor the meat, whether purchased or hunted, in a big way. To assist with this, I have developed three recipes for each major cut of whitetail; though all recipes herein work with farm raised steer, lamb, pork, or wild game (venison, elk, buffalo, caribou). Experiment with cut and recipe combinations to find your favorites. My version of Tafelspitz is presented as a soup in the 'for the Omnivores' chapter herein.

Chapter 1: For the CARNIVORES

- You've Got Game! Now what?
- From the Field to your Freezer
- Feasting: Recipes According to Venison Cut
  - BACKSTRAPS
    - Bordeaux Backstraps
    - Leek Filled Love Letters
    - Moroccan Harissa Backstrap Tagine
  - TENDERLOINS
    - Tender Loins
    - Venison Loin Black Bean Chili Verde
    - Smoky Chipotle Tenderloin Kabobs
  - FLANK STEAKS
    - The Easiest Dinner Ever
    - Cuban Mojo Venison Nestled in Whole Wheat Tortillas
    - Mongolian Venison Stir-Fry
  - LONDON BROIL – Top Round
    - Jalapeño Infused Broiled Kabobs
    - Kung Pao! Venison
    - Venison Broil Braised in Courvoisier
  - RUMP ROAST
    - Fall-Apart Venison Goulash
    - Venison Roast and Root Veggies in a Tomato Wine Reduction
    - 17 Pepper Venison Chili
  - STEW MEAT
    - Venison Bourguignon
    - The Full Treatment Venison Soup
    - Star Anise Perfumed Venison in a Potato Kale Stew
  - GROUND VENISON
    - Venison Cali Burgers
    - Classic Venison Tacos
    - Venison Bolognese
  - VENISON JERKY – three ways

The earliest recorded book of the Bible, Genesis, highlights the importance of archery, hunting, and venison. Read Genesis for the complete story on a dying father's last wish for tasty venison.

And these are the generations of Isaac, Abraham's son: Abraham begat Isaac: And Isaac was forty years old when he took Rebekah to wife. And Isaac intreated the Lord for his wife, because she was barren, and the Lord was intreated of him, and Rebekah his wife conceived. And the children struggled together within her; and she said, If it be so, why am I thus? And the Lord said unto her, Two nations are in thy womb; and the one people shall be stronger than the other people; and the elder shall serve the younger. And when her days to be delivered were fulfilled, behold, there were twins in her womb.

~ Genesis 25:19-24 KJV

And the boys grew: and Esau was a **cunning hunter**, a man of the field; and Jacob was a plain man, dwelling in tents. And **Isaac loved Esau, because he did eat of his venison**: but Rebekah loved Jacob.

~ Genesis 25:27-28 KJV

And it came to pass, that when Isaac was old, and his eyes were dim, so that he could not see, he called Esau his eldest son, and said unto him, My son: Behold now, I am old, I know not the day of my death: Now therefore **take, I pray thee, thy weapons**, thy quiver and thy bow, and go out to the field, **and take me some venison**; and make me some savoury meat, such as I love, and bring it to me, that I may eat; that my soul may bless thee before I die.

~ Genesis 27:1-4 KJV

And Jacob said unto to his father, I am Esau thy first born; I have done according as thou badest me: arise, I pray thee, **sit and eat of my venison**, that thy soul may bless me. And Isaac said unto his son, How is it that thou hast found it so quickly, my son?

~ Genesis 27:19-20 KJV

Even on his deathbed, Isaac knew that hunting, processing, and cooking venison would be tough to do within a few hours. Dressing your own deer is very rewarding; and a simple method follows to get you started.

You've Got Game! Now what?

Be Patient – Wait for your best shot for a quick recovery. If you see the deer "donkey kick" after the shot, you have more than likely hit the vitals. Congratulations!

Be Patient – After the kill, don't pressure an animal that is not in sight. Let it lie for a few hours to prevent an unnecessary run, and then track the blood trail.

Say Thank You and Field Dress – Honor your deer with a moment of silence and give thanks. Gut it where it lies to lighten your load, remove bacteria, and feed rodents.

Check Your Tag – Tear off your game tag before you transport your kill, then check it in at your nearest game check station, over the phone, or online.

Hang, Age and Process, or See Your Local Butcher – Leaving processing to the professionals supports local business and can maximize meat from your kill.

Visit your Local Taxidermist – Besides the dinner table, there is no better way to showcase your whitetail as a wall mount or deer skin rug.

From the Field to Your Freezer

But you shall not eat flesh with its life, that is, its blood.

~ Genesis 9:4 NKJV

Step One: Field Dressing

Regardless of outdoor temperatures, the first step is to remove the organs, stomach, etc., which is commonly referred to as gutting the deer. A sharp knife or preferably one with a gut hook should be utilized to open the cavity to avoid puncturing the stomach (i.e. paunch). This can be a daunting task for first time hunters so it helps to have an experienced hunter show you the ropes on the first one. There are also a myriad of step-by-step instructions and video demonstrations on the World Wide Web (i.e. Internet) that can assist you with steps such as cutting the diaphragm and windpipe, which are essential for easy removal of the organs/guts from the cavity.

Step Two: Hang Out - Cool the Meat & Drain the Blood

Following field dressing, the deer is ready to be transported to the local butcher for processing. However, many hunters prefer to perform the processing themselves, which is relatively easy to do and quite satisfying when you have been involved in every step from the kill to the dinner table. If you choose to process the deer yourself, then you will need a means to hang it, to facilitate removal of the hide and meat. A hanger, which is also referred to as a gambrel and pulley system, is an essential tool needed to complete these tasks. First, hang the deer head down. To do this, cut a slit on each back leg between the tendons to accommodate the use of the gambrel. Note hanging the deer head down allows the blood to drain away from the various cuts, which helps to minimize contact with any contaminants in the residual blood. If outdoor temperatures will not exceed the low 40s, then it is acceptable to leave the hide on and let the animal hang for a few days to facilitate blood draining and breakdown of lactic acid in the muscles. However, immediate hide removal is essential for temperatures above this threshold to allow the meat to cool. Hide removal beings at the hindquarters and trends toward the head of the animal. As noted before, an experienced hunter and/or tutorials via the Internet can assist you with this process, which is not hard to complete once you get the hang of it.

Step Three: Meat Removal

Once the deer is skinned out, you are ready to begin removal of the various cuts. A fixed or fold out table staged proximate to the hanging system will greatly facilitate temporary staging of the removed cuts, which helps to minimize contact with any potential contaminants such as soil, leaves, etc.

The first steps are removal of the "choice" or "prime" cuts, which are often referred to as the backstraps/tenderloins and hanging tenderloins. The backstraps parallel the top of spinal column, and the two hanging tenderloins are under the spine (i.e. cavity interior) in the pelvic region of the deer. Following removal of the "choice" cuts; you are ready to detach the hindquarters from the carcass. In our opinion, cutting through bone with a saw is an unnecessary step for removal of the hindquarters. We detach the hindquarters from the carcass by separating the femur bone balls from each pelvic socket. A stout knife blade and/or flat head screwdriver will facilitate the removal of the balls from the respective pelvic sockets. Each hindquarter contains a rump roast, haunch or round roast, and sirloin cut. Placing each hindquarter on the table, with the exterior side facing up, allows for easy deboning of the meat. You will notice a prominent "white line" that represents a "muscle flap" that separates the sirloin from the rump roast. Use the tip of a very sharp knife to start slowly slicing along this white line and keep the cut shallow! If done correctly, you will be separating the sirloin cut away from the rump roast and exposing the round roast. The round roast is removed by cutting it away from the underside of the femur bone. At this point you are ready to remove the rump roast by working your knife around the exposed femur bone down to the joint.

The shoulder and neck meat is also easily boned out directly from the carcass. We typically cube the shoulder and neck meat to facilitate the use of a meat grinder to make ground venison for burgers, sausage, meat spaghetti sauce, etc. We typically do not utilize the rib meat, but that decision is up to the individual. We temporarily store the meat in Ziploc bags and keep it refrigerated until we are ready for final processing.

Step Four: Fillet

If you hunt with a firearm, take extra care to remove any lead or shot. You do not need to be an expert butcher to filet your own cuts of venison. Just be willing to accept that your filets may never look as good as those from an expert; and you may not salvage as much meat as a professional would. Key items to filleting at home follow. Use a super sharp knife, as it will do the work for you. A dull knife requires more pressure and leads to a greater chance of injury. Follow the sinew (white fibers) with your fingers and gently stretch sections apart with one hand, while making small cuts using the knife with the other hand. Cut away as much sinew and fat from the large sections of meat as possible and you will end up with filets that look better than those shown in this chapter. Note that you are in charge. Eat what you like. Reserve unenticing pieces for the land as other animals will eat them. Trim away thin sections that are overly brown from aging, or that don't look or feel appetizing. This takes practice, but after time, you will be able to easily distinguish the tender cuts of thick meat relative to thin chewy flaps of muscle.

Step Five: Preserve

Our favorite method for preserving venison is the vacuum sealer. We have eaten venison up to two years old using this method. Rolls of heat sealable bags can be cut to the desired length to minimize waste, and the bags areas to label with Sharpie pens. Identify each bag with: 1) the sex (buck or doe), the date (month/day/year), and the type of filet (tenderloin, etc.). The worst method of preservation is unlined tin foil. Alternate methods include combinations of saran wrap, freezer bags, and freezer paper; labeled with indelible ink or pen on freezer tape.

Step Six: Thaw

Remove venison from the freezer and allow it to thaw within its airtight freezer bag in the sink, just in case the bag has a puncture. Frozen venison can be thawed in the refrigerator overnight slowly or at room temperature. Small cuts (less than one lb) will be ready within 2 - 4 hr; and larger roasts or cuts (greater than one lb) can take up to 8 hours. If you forgot to remove it from the freezer, fill a large stock or deep sauté pot with warm water and place the venison in its freezer bag in the water. Place a lid or something heavy on top of the venison to keep it from floating to the surface. Allow warm water to run into the pot until it reaches a lukewarm equilibrium. Most cuts of venison will be ready within 15 min to 1 hr using this method. Avoid thawing venison for excessively long periods of time in very warm climates to prevent spoiling. Use common sense. If something smells bad, discard it, as you would with any other food.

~ Chris Lalli

Feasting: Recipes According to Venison Cut
BACKSTRAPS

Bordeaux Backstraps

Sear, Oven Roast, and Deglaze

For the Venison

- 1 backstrap, ~1 lb, cut in half
- 2 tsp sea salt
- 20 grinds of black pepper
- 2 Tbs olive oil
- 8 garlic cloves, peel and trim
- 4 sprigs of fresh herbs (rosemary and or thyme)
- ½ cup red wine, for oven roast, try Bordeaux
- ½ cup red wine, for deglazing

Details: Preheat oven to 380 °F (roast); see Lessons on deglazing, page 253

- Season both sides of backstraps with sea salt and pepper
- Heat olive oil in a sauté pan (pan must be oven and stovetop safe for roasting and deglazing) over high heat until shimmering (just below the smoking point)
- Add the backstraps and garlic cloves to the shimmering oil
- Sear the backstraps for ~2 min on one side, or until they naturally release upon a vigorous shake; when you can easily flip them, turn them over
- Add the herb sprigs and ½ cup of wine to the venison; shake the pan to blend
- Transfer the pan to the upper third of the oven and roast for 7 - 8 min until the thickest part of the backstraps reaches 120 - 125 °F (longer for larger fillets)
- Remove the pan from the oven, and transfer the backstraps to a cutting board
- Add the second ½ cup of wine to the garlic and herbs; adjust the heat to high
- Scrape up the caramelized browned bits with a wooden spoon to deglaze the pan and incorporate into sauce; reduce the sauce by about half to a thickened au jus
- Lightly press the roasted garlic cloves into the finished sauce to incorporate their flavor, while keeping them whole to serve on each slice of venison

NOTE: Gourmet restaurants garner high prices for this dish; yet succulent backstraps can be prepared at home in < 15 min thanks to wine's tenderizing effect. Red Bordeaux wines (pronounced: boar-doe) are produced in the Bordeaux region of France; and are typically blends of wine grapes such as: Cabernet Sauvignon, Cabernet Franc, and Merlot. Deglazing the au jus over high heat burns off the alcohol and softens the garlic cloves. Larger backstraps and increase roasting time softens cloves further.

Backstraps

Leek Filled Love Letters

Sauté, Fill, Tie, Roast, and Deglaze

For the Venison
- 2 backstraps, butterfly each in thirds or halves, ~ 1.5 lbs
- 1 Tbs sea salt
- 10 grinds of black pepper

For the Sautéed Leek Filling
- 2 Tbs of olive oil
- 2 Tbs of butter
- 2 leeks, white and tender green portion, minced
- 1 Tbs sea salt
- 10 grinds of black pepper
- 1 tsp red pepper flakes
- 3 garlic cloves, minced
- ½ cup white wine
- juice of 1 lemon
- 2 Tbs of heavy cream
- ½ cup white wine

Details: Preheat oven to 380 °F (roast); see Lessons on deglazing, page 253
- Heat olive oil and butter in a sauté pan over high heat until butter is bubbling
- Add the leeks, salt, and pepper, sauté on high for ~ 4 min
- Reduce the heat to med-high, add the pepper flakes and garlic, and sauté for an additional ~ 4 min; leeks should retain their bright green color and be tender
- Add ½ cup of wine to deglaze; remove pan from heat; stir in lemon and cream
- Butterfly the backstraps; cut in thirds to yield a thin piece of meat that can be rolled; rub with salt and pepper; and top with a thick layer of the sautéed leeks
- Fold the filled filets like a love letter, in thirds, and tie with five pieces of twine
- Transfer the filled venison to a roasting pan (oven and stovetop safe)
- Roast at 380 °F for ~ 45 min; remove from oven; transfer love letters to a plate
- Add ½ cup wine to the roasting pan, deglaze caramelized leek char over high heat
- Slice love letters to show filling, and finish with deglazed caramelized leek sauce

NOTE: As you work through this cookbook, you may notice it is missing something. I do not like white onions; although I love leeks, scallions, and garlic. Mincing leeks can be daunting your first time. First, slice off the bottom root and tough green tops at an angle, as shown. Then, slice the leeks in half vertically, rinse the dirt away, and mince.

Backstraps

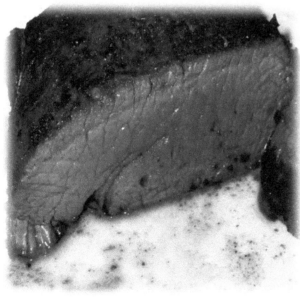

Moroccan Harissa Backstrap Tagine

Sear, and Steam on Stovetop in Tagine (or covered sauté pan)

For the Moroccan Rubbed Venison

- 2 small backstraps, each cut in half, ~1.5 lbs total
- 1 tsp sea salt
- 1 Tbs of Moroccan rub

For the Moroccan Tagine (see Pantry for olives, page 262)

- 2 Tbs olive oil
- ½ cup pitted Kalamata olives

Harissa Stew Sauce, *optional*

- See the following two pages for recipe and details

Details:

- Coat the backstraps with the salt and Moroccan spice rub
- Heat olive oil in Tagine base (or cast iron pan) over high heat until shimmering
- Sear the backstraps for ~1 ~ 2 min on each side
- Reduce the heat to low; add the olives and optional Harissa sauce
- Place Tagine or lid on cast iron base; steam on stovetop for ~10 - 12 min
- Serve, with or without sauce, and olives per the Note and opposite photo

NOTE: Moroccan spice blends, such as Ras El Hanout, can be purchased at the grocery store; or, you can blend your own with roughly equal parts: cumin, cayenne pepper, turmeric, paprika, cinnamon, ginger, cloves, and cardamom. If you are pressed for time, or just don't love spicy food, skip the sauce. Venison seared with a simple rub is equally delicious as long as it is not overcooked (see photo at left).

NOTE on Tagine ~ You Don't Need One, but you may Want One:
My Tagine was an awesome gift. I love its beauty, heavy cast iron base for searing, and inimitable gentle yet powerful steaming capability. The dimple on the top holds an ice cube that condenses rising steam from the venison. The conical shape coerces the condensate to drip back down into the dish and results in unbelievably tender meat. Tagines also allow for oven-free evenings in the summertime.

Roasting Red Peppers and Harissa

Sweat Skin off of Blackened Peppers in a Paper Bag for Easy Removal

Roasting Red Peppers and Harissa

Stove Top Sear, Bag Steam, and Blender

For the Harissa (see Pantry for red chili peppers, page 262)

- 1 Tbs olive oil
- 3 garlic cloves, peel and trim
- 3 red peppers, roasted
- 2 dried red chili peppers

- 2 Tbs white wine vinegar
- juice of 1 lemon
- 1 tsp sea salt
- 1 tsp cumin, *optional*

Details: see Lessons on peppers and capsaicin, page 253

- Heat the olive oil in a cast iron or heavy pan over high heat until shimmering
- Add the garlic cloves, red peppers, and chili peppers; blacken the red peppers (literally) for ~ 2 - 3 min on each side until blistering
- Remove the garlic and chilies after one turn; reserve to prevent overcooking
- Transfer the red peppers to a paper or plastic bag; seal shut for ~ 10 min to sweat the skin off; remove the peppers from the bag and loosen the skin away
- Remove the cores and seeds from peppers to taste; tear chilies into small pieces
- Add the garlic, peppers, chilies, vinegar, lemon, salt, and cumin to a blender; puree for 1 - 2 min until the chili peppers are incorporated into a smooth sauce

NOTE on Roasting Red Peppers:

Store bought roasted red peppers are very expensive and leftover peppers mold in the jar after a few days. Roasting your own is easy; though I hadn't tried until recently as I thought you needed an open flame. You don't. Even though I have a gas burner now, I roasted mine in the pan, and it worked great. It was also amusing to burn food and feel good about it for a change. Just remember to use the vent.

NOTE on Harissa: Have a Cold – Eat Harissa

Harissa sauce is packed with vitamin C. One cup of chopped red chili or bell peppers packs more than 300% of the daily recommended amount of vitamin C, relative to 50 or 85% for 1 lemon or orange, respectively. Lemons also offer antibacterial, anti-viral, and immune boosting powers. Recent university studies have also found that garlic may help prevent cancer and heart disease.

TENDERLOINS

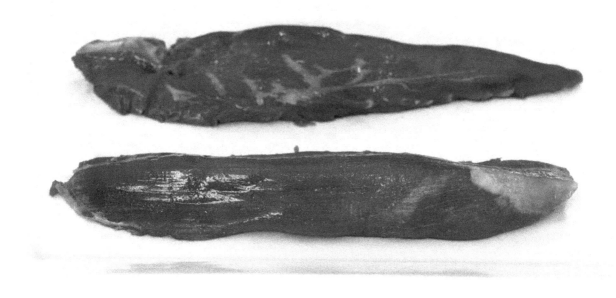

49

Tender Loins

Sear, Oven Roast, and Deglaze

For the Venison
- 1 tenderloin, ~1 lb, cut in half
- 1 - 2 tsp sea salt
- 10 grinds of black pepper
- 2 Tbs olive oil
- ½ cup of red wine, beef broth, or fruit juice; or use ¼ cup of red wine vinegar, try balsamic or sherry

Details: Preheat oven to 380 °F (roast); see Lessons on deglazing, page 253
- Halve the tenderloin if it is too long for the pan; rub with salt and pepper; heat olive oil in a sauté pan (oven and stovetop safe) over high heat until shimmering
- Sear tenderloins for ~1 min on each side
- Place pan in the upper third of the oven, and roast for ~ 8 - 10 min until the thickest part of the backstraps reaches 120 – 125 °F
- Remove the pan from oven, and transfer the tenderloins to a plate
- Add deglazing liquid of choice to pan over high heat; incorporate the caramelized bits into au jus with a wooden spoon; remove from heat upon desired consistency
- Pour thickened au jus over tenderloins and serve

NOTE:

This recipe is the perfect example of keeping it simple. When you have a great cut of venison, salt and pepper may be all you need for flavor. Tenderloins are so inherently tender; you do not need the wine for tenderizing. Though, if you would like to dress the dish up with sauce, try deglazing a pan sauce rather than using store bought steak sauce. Here, you may use your favorite red wine, broth, fruit glaze, or even a good vinegar, such as sherry or balsamic. If you are unsure how to select wine, look for a bottle that costs between $5 and $20 and that has a rating of 85 or higher (100 is the highest score). Wine cellars and grocery stores typically list wine scores, making your selection simple. For a special occasion, try Amarone, or Amarone della Valpolicella. These Italian wines are expensive (starting around $40), though intensely flavored, dry, rich, and lush. Treat Amarone with care. Sip it slowly and share it with good friends.

Romans 14:3 Dinner Party

Dinner Salad for the Omnivores

Dinner Salad for the Vegetarians

Tender Loins with Baby Greens

Sear, Oven Roast, and Add to Greens

Venison Dinner Salad: Serves 3 to 4
- Venison Tender Loins Recipe, ~1 lb

For the Baby Greens Salad
- 4 cups mache rosettes
- 2 cups arugula
- 4 oz goat cheese
- 3 Tbs pine nuts
- ½ cup cherry tomatoes, halved

Salad Dressing, *Optional*
- 1 ~ 2 garlic cloves, chopped
- 1 tsp salt + 20 grinds of pepper
- ⅓ cup balsamic vinegar
- ¼ cup olive oil
- 1 tsp fresh rosemary, chopped

Details:
- Prepare Venison Tender Loins recipe (page 50) with salt and pepper; no deglazing is necessary. Let the venison rest for ~ 5 min; slice into 2" thick pieces
- Wash and spin dry the mache rosettes (lettuce) and arugula; add to salad bowls
- Top the greens with crumbled goat cheese, pine nuts, and cherry tomatoes
- Add the garlic, salt, pepper, vinegar, oil and fresh herbs (try 1 tsp rosemary or 6 basil leaves) to a blender; blend on high, ~ 2 min, until the garlic is pulverized
- Top the salads with the sliced venison tenderloin and dressing; or simply splash the salad with olive oil, your favorite vinegar, salt, and pepper

NOTE: See Romans 14:3, NCV

A big salad is a great base for a dinner party to satisfy all guests, especially when your guests may be a mix of carnivores, vegetarians, or vegans unbeknownst to you. By preparing a simple base of fresh ingredients, guests can choose their main item to top the salad off with. Omnivores can choose from venison, sautéed goat cheese or tofu medallions. Vegetarians and vegans may opt for the latter two. First, dredge ½" thick slices of goat cheese or tofu in breadcrumbs; then sauté in 2 Tbs of olive oil until golden. Do this quickly, ~ 30 sec on each side, to prevent the cheese from melting. Add roasted red peppers and Kalamata olives (page 262) for a more robust vegetarian meal. Start off with a soup or grain side dish, and you'll have a complete well-balanced meal for all.

Tenderloins

My Favorite

Venison Loin Black Bean Chili Verde

Stove Top Dutch Oven Stew

For the Venison
- 4 – 5 tenderloins, ~1.5 lbs total
- 2 + 2 Tbs of olive oil
- 2 tsp sea salt + 10 grinds of pepper

For the Black Beans
- 1 cup of dried black beans
- 4 cups water
- 2 Tbs olive oil + 2 bay leaves

Green Pepper Bowl
4 poblano peppers
2 banana peppers
3 jalapeño peppers
3 Serrano peppers

Tomatillos Bowl
15 – 20 tomatillos
10 garlic cloves, minced
1 Tbs salt
30 grinds black pepper

Accouterments
2 Tbs white wine vinegar
juice of 1 lime
⅓ cup of cilantro leaves
Paranno cheese, grated

Details: see Lessons on peppers and capsaicin, page 253
- Cut the tenderloins into ~2" cubes, and toss with salt and pepper
- Pressure cook the black beans and bay leaves in water and oil for 25 min and drain; alternatively, soak the beans overnight and simmer for 1 - 2 hr, or use canned beans
- Remove pepper cores and seeds to your taste from each of the peppers; dice the poblano and bananas into ½" pieces; dice the jalapeño and Serranos into ¼" pieces
- Remove the tomatillo skins under running water; slice ~2" pieces off of the core, and discard the cores; add garlic, salt, and pepper to the Tomatillos Bowl
- Heat 2 Tbs olive oil in a Dutch oven over high heat; brown venison ~2 min, each side
- Transfer venison to a bowl; heat 2 more Tbs olive oil over high in the Dutch oven
- Add the contents of the Green Pepper Bowl to the Dutch oven; sauté for ~5 min
- Add the contents of the Tomatillos Bowl to the Dutch oven; sauté for another 5 min
- Reduce the heat to low, stir in the venison, cover, and steep for ~1 hr over low heat, stirring occasionally, until the peppers and tomatillos have melded into a thick stew
- Add the black beans, vinegar, and lime juice to the Dutch oven; remove from heat
- Add cilantro and grated Parrano cheese to each individual bowl upon serving

NOTE: Inspiration here came from Roaring Fork's Pork Chili Verde in Scottsdale, AZ. We prefer venison. Our friends, Eric and Laura Robinson, introduced us to nutty Parrano cheese. It is a Holland blend of Dutch Gouda and Italian Parmigiano Reggiano.

Tenderloins

Smoky Chipotle Tenderloin Kabobs

Marinate and Grill

For the Venison Marinade
- 2 – 3 venison tenderloins, ~ 1.5 lb total, ~2" cubes
- ⅓ cup olive oil, or any infused olive oil
- ⅓ cup of unfiltered apple cider vinegar, or favorite vinegar
- 1 Tbs sea salt
- 2 Tbs of favorite dried chili seasoning
- 1 Tbs of dried chipotle pepper flakes, or powder
- 1 tsp of Dijon mustard
- 4 – 5 garlic cloves, crushed or chopped

Details: Preheat grill with a med-high flame
- Slice the tenderloins into large, evenly sized ~2" cubes
- Whisk the remaining marinade ingredients in a large bowl and add the venison; cover and marinate for at least 30 min at room temp or up to 8 hr in the fridge
- Preheat the grill with a med-high flame; spear ~ 5 – 6 venison cubes on each skewer; grill one side of the venison for ~ 4 – 5 min with the lid closed
- Nudge the kebabs and when they release with slight pressure, flip them over, pour on remaining marinade, and grill for another 4 – 5 min. Use caution here. The oil in the marinade will cause flames to leap from the grill; this step will caramelize the kabobs and make you look like a grill master

NOTE on Marinade:

I love marinades, as almost anything goes. Simply blend your favorite oil, vinegar, and citrus juice with salt, pepper, dried spices, fresh herbs, garlic, peppers, mustard, or honey. Any dried spices work here, although Smoky Paprika Chipotle and Texas Red spice blends from Victoria Gourmet are exceptional (see Resources, page 266). Her Chipotle and Jalapeño Pepper Flakes are incomparable. I use a small whisk to grab ~ 2 tsp of Dijon mustard directly from the jar and mix it in to emulsify the blend. Organic Apple Cider vinegar tastes delicious and reduces cholesterol levels. Leeks, onions, shallots, or a blend thereof, could supplant or add to the garlic. You've got options.

FLANK STEAK

The Easiest Dinner Ever

Quick Marinade and Grill

For the Grilled Flank Steak
- 1 flank steak, ~1 lb
- 1 Tbs salt
- 30 grinds of black pepper
- ~ ½ cup of favorite store bought or homemade marinade
  - our favorite store bought is A.1.® New York Steakhouse

Details: Preheat grill with a med-high flame
- Coat both sides of the flank steak with salt, pepper, and marinade
- Let this sit for at least 10 min, or up to ~ 45 min at room temp
- Preheat the grill with a med-high flame
- Grill one side of the steak until it releases from the grates easily with a slight nudge, ~ 5 – 6 min; turn, and grill the other side for another 4 - 5 min
- Remove the flank steak from grill and let it sit for ~5 min before carving

NOTE:

This is the easiest dinner ever since the prep time is less than 5 minutes, and my husband does all the grilling. My main job is to remember to take the flank steak out of the freezer to thaw before work. This dish is a fine example of how the quality of the venison, rather than the final preparation, dictates the flavor and texture. When processed, stored, and thawed properly, venison is juicier and more flavorful than most red meats even though it has nearly zero fat. There is no need to pickle tender cuts of venison for hours in highly acidic marinades. The A1 brand marinades are our favorite as their viscosity sticks to the venison throughout the entire grill.

To rest or not to rest?

Cutting into cooked meat immediately upon removal from the heat source typically results in the release of its natural juices. The amount of juice retained within the meat, or its "juiciness", increases with resting time. Whether you can wait for this step or not, the natural juice works as a great finishing sauce.

Flank Steak

Cuban Mojo Venison Nestled in Whole Wheat Tortillas

Quick Marinade, Grill, and Taco Assembly

For the Venison
- 2 flank steaks, ~1.5 lbs total
- 2 tsp salt + black pepper

For the Mojo Marinade: mix together and reserve ⅓ cup
- 3 garlic cloves, minced
- 2 Tbs white wine vinegar
- 2 Tbs cilantro leaves, minced
- 1 Serrano pepper, ⅛" dice
- juice of 2 limes
- juice of ½ lemon
- juice of 1 orange
- 2 Tbs olive oil

For the Sauce
- ⅓ cup reserved mojo
- 1 Tbs pureed chipotle adobo*
- 2 Tbs cilantro leaves, minced
- 5 Tbs sour cream

Toppings
- cherry tomatoes, diced
- 1 red bell pepper, sautéed
- iceberg lettuce, shredded
- jack cheese, grated

Details: Preheat grill with a med-high flame
- Marinate the flank steak in the mojo marinade for 30 min to 1 hr
- Preheat a grill with a med-high flame; grill the flank steaks ~4 - 5 min on each side, let them rest ~ 5 min; slice into ½" wide strips
- Top whole wheat soft taco shells (page 180) with Venison, Sauce, and Toppings

NOTE:

This recipe is similar to The Easiest Dinner Ever. Here, store bought marinade is replaced with a fresh Cuban Mojo marinade, and the grilled venison is coupled with a citrusy cilantro cream sauce and your favorite taco accouterments. Canned chipotles in adobo sauce* are one of my favorite produce items as it adds an unmistakably spicy smoky flavor to any dish. It can be found in most grocery stores, or many gourmet stores (see Pantry, page 262). Pureeing the sauce lessens the potential for a bite into an onion or seed. If using a low speed blender, deseed the chipotles before pureeing.

Flank Steak

Gingered Leeks and Scallions Perfectly Compliment the Piquant Venison

Mongolian Venison Stir-Fry

Quick Marinade and Stir-Fry

For the Venison Marinade & Sear
- 1 flank, ~ 1 lb, ~ 1" x ¼" strips
- 2 tsp ginger, finely grated
- 2 Tbs low sodium soy sauce
- 2 tsp corn starch
- 2 Tbs water
- 2 Tbs peanut oil – to sear

For the Vegetables
- 1 Tbs peanut oil – to sear
- 1 leek, tender portions, halved lengthwise, 2" pieces
- 2 bunches of green onions; green portions, 1" pieces; white portions, ¼" pieces

For the Sauce (see Pantry for sauces, page 262)
- 2 tsp ginger, finely grated
- 4 Tbs low sodium soy sauce
- 1 Tbs hoisin sauce
- 1 Tbs of chili bean sauce, or favorite Szechuan sauce
- 1 Tbs Chinese rice wine (Shaoxing wine), or dry sherry
- 1 Tbs Chinese black rice vinegar, or balsamic vinegar
- 2 tsp corn starch

Details:
- Whisk the ginger, soy sauce, corn starch and water together; add the flank steak; marinate for ~ 30 min while preparing the Vegetables and Sauce Bowls
- Heat 2 Tbs peanut oil in a wok over high heat until shimmering, swirl to coat wok; stir-fry the venison for ~ 3 min on each side until the pink color disappears
- Transfer the venison to a plate, and add another 1 Tbs peanut oil to the wok
- Add the leeks and green peppers to the wok and stir-fry for ~ 2 min; cover and steam the vegetables for ~ 1 min; remove cover, return venison to the wok
- Whisk the contents of the Sauce once more to blend the corn starch; add to the wok, toss all to mix; turn off the heat after ~1 min; allow sauce to thicken, ~ 2 min
- Serve over brown or sweet brown rice

NOTE: This is my recreation of my husband's favorite dish from a major Asian chain restaurant. We live in a small college town nearby VA Tech. Though lacking major chain restaurants and reliable Internet, our town is full of school spirit, cool local eateries, rolling hills, fantastic fly fishing, great hunting, and zero traffic.

LONDON BROIL

Jalapeño Infused Broiled Kabobs

Quick Marinade and Oven Broil

For the Venison Marinade
- 1 venison broil, ~ 1.5 lbs
- ⅓ cup olive oil
- ½ cup apple cider vinegar
- 5 garlic cloves, minced
- 1 Tbs salt + 30 grinds pepper
- 1 Tbs Italian seasoning
- 2 Tbs jalapeño flakes
- 2 tsp Dijon mustard

For the Vegetable Roasting Pan ~ vegetables cut into 2" pieces
- ½ head of broccoli
- 1 yellow squash
- 1 zucchini
- 1 red pepper
- 1 green pepper
- ~ 4 Tbs olive oil
- 2 tsp sea salt
- 20 grinds of black pepper

Fennel Tzatziki Dipping Sauce (whisk all ingredients together)
- 1 Tbs champagne vinegar
- juice of ½ lemon
- 2 tsp fennel seeds, chopped
- 1 garlic clove, chopped
- 1 Tbs sea salt
- 20 grinds of black pepper
- 1 Tbs of olive oil
- 1 hot house cucumber, unpeeled, deseeded, ¼" dice
- 8 oz of Greek yogurt

Details: Preheat oven to (broil) for venison; reduce to 400 °F (roast) for vegetables
- Slice the venison broil into ~2" cubes; whisk marinade ingredients together and add the venison; marinate for 30 min at room temp or up to 4 hr in fridge
- Add the vegetables to a roasting pan and drizzle with oil; top with salt and pepper; place the pan on the middle rack of the oven (in broil mode)
- Skewer ~ 6 venison cubes on each spear; place on broiler pan on top oven rack
- Broil the venison for ~ 4 min, flip, pour remaining marinade on, broil ~ 3 more min
- Remove the venison from the oven and reduce the oven to 400 °F
- Continue roasting the vegetables another 10 min while you whisk the Tzatziki dip

NOTE: The vegetable recipe is included here to complete a meal for those that do not have a grill or don't like grilling outside in the rain or snow.

London Broil

This Dish is as Spicy and Tasty as it is Colorful and Textured

Kung Pao! Venison

Quick Marinade and Stir-Fry

For the Venison Marinade (see Pantry for red chili peppers, page 262)

- 1 broil, 1.5 lb, ½" thick strips
- 2 tsp corn starch
- 2 Tbs low sodium soy sauce

- 3 dried red chili peppers, torn into small pieces, deseeded
- 2 Tbs peanut oil – to sear

For the Vegetables & Peanuts

- 1 Tbs peanut oil – to sear
- 2 red peppers, 1" pieces

- 1 green pepper, 1" pieces
- ½ cup dry roasted peanuts

For the Sauce (see Pantry for sauces, page 262)

- 2 tsp corn starch
- 2 Tbs black bean garlic sauce
- 1 Tbs chili garlic sauce
- 2 tsp hoisin sauce

- 2 Tbs Chinese black rice vinegar, or balsamic vinegar
- ½ cup favorite broth, or water
- 4 Tbs low sodium soy sauce

Details: see Lessons on peppers and capsaicin, page 253

- Whisk the corn starch, soy sauce, and chili peppers together; add the sliced broil; marinate for ~ 30 min while preparing the Vegetables, Peanuts, and Sauce Bowls
- Heat 2 Tbs peanut oil in a wok over high heat until shimmering, swirl to coat wok
- Stir-fry the venison for ~ 3 min on each side until the pink color disappears
- Transfer the venison to a plate; add 1 Tbs peanut oil to the wok
- Add the red and green peppers to the peanut oil; stir-fry for ~ 2 min; cover to steam peppers for ~ 1 min until crisp tender; return venison to wok; add peanuts
- Whisk the contents of the Sauce once more; add to the wok, toss to mix; turn off the heat after ~1 min; allow sauce to thicken ~ 2 min and serve over brown rice

NOTE: The peanuts and chili peppers provide the Kung and Pao! You might wear gloves while tearing the dried peppers, as they are fiery hot. With a few stocked Asian base sauces, and a jar of dry roasted peanuts, this dish can be made any night, with any vegetable (sliced carrots, broccoli, etc.). Chili sauce, or chili garlic sauce, can be used here. Popular choices include Sriracha and Sambal Oelek. If you can't find black bean garlic sauce, use any Chinese bean or soybean sauce, or even miso paste.

London Broil

Courvoisier Tenderizes and Lends a Mildly Sweet Sophisticated Aroma

Venison Broil Braised in Courvoisier

Quick Sear and Oven Braise

For the Venison
- 1 venison broil, ~ 1.5 lbs
- 2 tsp sea salt
- 30 grinds of black pepper

For the Roasting Pan
- 2 Tbs olive oil
- 4 carrots, peeled, halved lengthwise and crosswise
- ½ lb green beans, ends trimmed
- ½ + ¼ cups of Courvoisier®

Details: Preheat oven to 380 °F (roast); see Lessons on deglazing, page 253
- Coat both sides of the venison broil with salt and pepper
- Heat olive oil in a stovetop/oven safe sauté pan over high heat until shimmering
- Sear the broil on one side for ~ 2 min, shake pan to loosen the venison; when it can be easily turned, flip the broil to the other side, sear another ~ 1 min
- Add the carrots, green beans, and ½ cup of Courvoisier to the pan
- Transfer the pan to the upper third rack in the oven and roast for ~ 10 – 15 min until the meat reaches 120 °F in the thickest part (for medium-rare)
- Remove from the oven; transfer the meat to a cutting board; let it rest ~ 5 min
- While the venison is resting, return the pan back to the burner over high heat; add another ¼ cup of Courvoisier to the pan to deglaze
- Hold the pan handle with an oven mitt, and scrape the caramelized bits from the bottom with a wooden spoon to incorporate the sauce into the vegetables
- Carve the meat and serve with the roasted vegetables and sauce

NOTE:

Courvoisier is a fine French brandy produced in the town of Jarnac, using the finest ugni blanc grapes from the Cognac region of France. This recipe is similar to the Bordeaux backstraps, but with roasted vegetables and Courvoisier. It is a good example of cooking with what you have rather than running to the store to follow a recipe. Nearly any vegetable will work as a great base to soak up the au jus flavors. The alcohol burns off while deglazing and the flavors intermingle with the tender beef.

RUMP ROAST

Fall-Apart Venison Goulash

Pan Seared and Slow Cooked in Crock Pot

For the Venison
- 1 venison rump roast, ~ 2lbs
- 1 Tbs sea salt
- 30 grinds of black pepper
- 2 Tbs olive oil

For the Crock Pot
- 8 carrots, peeled, cut in half horizontally, then in thirds
- 2 Tbs of smoked paprika
- 1 head of garlic cloves, peeled, trimmed and chopped
- 1 bottle of red wine + ¾ cup of broth, or any 4 cup blend of broth, water, and or wine
- 28 oz can crushed tomatoes
- 1 Tbs sea salt

Details: (if your crock pot insert is not stove top safe, begin with a sauté pan)
- Coat the rump roast with salt and pepper
- Heat olive oil in a stovetop safe, crock pot insert (or sauté pan) over high heat until shimmering; sear the rump roast for about 1 min on each side; add the carrots, paprika, and roughly chopped garlic; sauté together for ~ 5 min
- Stir in the wine and broth; bring to a rapid simmer for 5 min to boil off the alcohol
- Add the crock pot insert to the crock, top with crushed tomatoes, salt, and stir
- Cover and slow cook on High Power for ~6 - 8 hr; pull meat apart with fork

NOTE:

The rump roast is a cut from the "bottom round" roast, or the lower section of the rear leg. While the "London Broil" is technically the name of a finished dish, it is typically prepared using the "top round" roast cut. Bottom rounds are lean, and somewhat tough; therefore benefit from long and slow roasts. In many side-by-side pressure cooker verses slow cooker experiments, I have found that the slow cooker results in fall-apart meat every time. This is a fantastic recipe to put together a few minutes before leaving for work or a Saturday hunt. In a pinch, skip the sautés and run. Either way, you will return to a home filled with a phenomenal aroma and the most buttery-tender meat imaginable. Add a chopped potato for a classic Viennese side street café stew.

Rump Roast

Mash the Tomatoes for a Stew or Leave Whole for Vibrant Color

Venison Roast and Root Veggies in a Tomato Wine Reduction

Pan Seared, Longer Roast and Poach

For the Venison

- 1 rump roast, ~1.5 lbs
- 2 Tbs olive oil
- 1 Tbs sea salt
- 30 grinds of black pepper

For the Pan

- 4 carrots and or parsnips, peeled, quartered
- 1 lb of baby potatoes, halved
- 10 garlic cloves, peel and trim
- 2 tsp salt + 20 grinds of pepper
- ½ cup red wine
- 28 oz can of whole tomatoes, San Marzano are best

Details: Preheat oven to 380 °F (roast)

- Rub the rump roast with salt and pepper
- Heat the olive oil in an oven and stovetop safe sauté pan over high heat until shimmering; sear the rump roast for ~1 min on each side until browned
- Add the carrots, potatoes, garlic cloves, salt, and pepper; sauté all for ~ 4 min
- Add the wine to deglaze; reduce the heat to low; add the whole tomatoes; stir gently, and transfer the pan in to the oven
- Roast for ~ 20 - 25 min until medium-rare (~ 125 °F in thickest part)
- Remove the pan from the oven and transfer the roast to a carving board to rest
- Return the sauté pan with vegetables to the stovetop; heat over high heat; lightly crush the tomatoes and roasted garlic cloves into the sauce with a fork for ~ 3 min
- Slice the venison and plate with roasted veggies and rustic garlic tomato sauce

NOTE: This is a great way to cook a roast, especially after work, when you don't have 8 hours to spare in the slow cooker. Note that no spices beyond salt and pepper are added here. You may keep it simple, or throw in any fresh herbs that you have in the fridge. The acidity from the tomato sauce (with a pH of ~ 4) tenderizes the roast, while the garlic, potatoes and carrots infuse the sauce with flavor and texture.

Rump Roast

Remove Some Membranes and Seeds from Peppers to Control the Spice

17 Pepper Venison Chili

Sauté and Dutch Oven

For the Venison
- 1 - 2 roasts, ~ 2.5 lbs, 2" cubes
- 2 tsp sea salt
- 30 grinds of black pepper
- 2 Tbs olive oil

For the Beans
- 1 cup dried red kidney beans
- 2 bay leaves
- 4 cups water
- 2 Tbs olive oil

For the Pepper Bowl
- 1 red pepper, 1" dice
- 1 green pepper, 1" dice
- 6 jalapeño peppers, ¼" dice
- 6 Serrano peppers, ¼" dice
- 3 chipotle peppers, ¼" dice
- 8 garlic cloves, minced
- 3 Tbs chili powder

For the Sauté and Simmer
- 2 Tbs olive oil
- ⅓ cup of favorite white wine
- 1 ½ Tbs salt
- 2 bay leaves
- 28 oz can crushed tomatoes
- 28 oz can whole tomatoes
- 3 ears of sweet corn kernels

Details: see Lessons on peppers and capsaicin, page 253
- Pressure cook the beans and bay leaves in water and oil on high for 25 min and drain; or, soak the beans overnight and simmer for 1 - 2 hr; or use canned beans
- Toss venison with salt and pepper; heat olive oil in a Dutch oven over high heat until shimmering; sauté venison in 2 batches until browned; transfer to a plate
- Deseed and dice peppers for the Pepper Bowl; top with garlic and chili powder
- Heat 2 Tbs of olive oil in the Dutch over high heat, sauté the Pepper Bowl contents ~ 3 min; stir in wine to deglaze ~ 30 sec; add salt, bay leaves, tomatoes and venison; cover; reduce heat to low; boil the corn cobs for ~ 3 min; slice off the kernels; add the corn and beans to the chili; simmer ~ 1 hr; see note for serving

NOTE: Top this hearty, juicy, spicy chili with diced avocado, cilantro, lime juice, and cheese to heighten the flavors and cool if desired. If you like it scorching hot, use some seeds and membranes from the chilies (I include 1 - 2 Serranos). For chili powder, I favor a combination of Honey Aleppo Pepper and Texas Red by Victoria Gourmet.

STEW MEAT

Venison Bourguignon

Sauté and Dutch Oven

For the Venison
- stew meat, ~2 lbs, 2" cubes
- 1 Tbs sea salt
- 30 grinds of black pepper
- 2 Tbs olive oil

For the Bourguignon
- 2 Tbs olive oil
- 3 carrots, peeled, ⅛" coins
- 1 onion, peeled, quartered
- 1 Tbs tomato paste
- 4 garlic cloves, minced
- 3 sprigs of thyme
- 2 bay leaves
- 2 Tbs whole wheat flour
- 2 cups beef broth
- 2 cups of Beaujolais wine

For the Mushrooms
- 1 lb baby portabellas, stems removed, quartered
- 2 Tbs olive oil
- 2 Tbs butter

Details: Preheat oven to 325 °F (roast)
- Coat the venison with salt and pepper; heat olive oil in a Dutch oven over high heat until shimmering; brown venison in 2 batches; transfer each batch to a plate
- Add the olive oil, carrots, onion, tomato paste, garlic, thyme, and bay leaves to the pot; sauté ~5 min, add the venison; sprinkle with flour; sauté ~ 1 min; stir in the broth and wine; bring to a simmer; cover; transfer to the oven; roast for 2 ½ hr
- Remove the pot from the oven; remove the beef and carrots with a slotted spoon
- Boil the sauce on the stovetop to thicken; return beef and carrots back to pot
- Heat the oil and butter in a sauté pan on high, sauté the mushrooms ~ 4 min until browned; stir the mushrooms into the stew; garnish with curly leaf parsley

NOTE: This French stew made famous by Julia Child is sublime. Her classic recipe includes peeled pearl onions. Here, a yellow onion melds into the stew, and venison imparts its delicious flavor. Browning the venison in batches ensures searing, rather than steaming due to overcrowding. Beaujolais (pronounced: bow-je-lay) is a light red wine produced from Gamay and Pinot Noir grapes in the Burgundy region of France.

Stew Meat

The Full Treatment Venison Soup

Stove Top Dutch Oven

For the Venison
- stew meat, ~2 lbs, 2" cubes
- 2 Tbs olive oil
- 1 Tbs sea salt
- 30 grinds of black pepper

For the Vegetable Sauté Bowl
- 2 Tbs olive oil
- 2 leeks, white and tender green portions, minced
- 10 garlic cloves, minced
- 1 Tbs sea salt, and pepper
- 2 stalks celery, ¼" slice
- 6 carrots, peeled, ¼" coins
- 10 baby gold potatoes, cut into thirds
- 1 head of fennel, core and outer skin removed, ¼" slice
- 1 cup broccoli, 1" pieces

For the Stew
- 2 ears sweet of corn kernels
- ¾ head of kale, chopped
- 1 cup green beans, halved
- 14 oz can diced tomatoes
- 1 bottle of Burgundy wine
- 8 cups water or broth

Details:
- Toss the venison with salt and pepper; heat 2 Tbs oil in a large stockpot over high heat until shimmering; sauté venison until browned ~ 3 min; transfer to a bowl
- Add 2 Tbs olive oil to the stockpot; sauté contents of the Vegetable Bowl ~5 min
- Boil corn cobs for ~ 3 min, slice off the kernels; add to the sautéed Vegetables
- Return the Venison to the stockpot with the vegetables, top with kale, green beans, tomatoes, wine, and broth; reduce heat to low; cover, and simmer for ~2 hr

NOTE: My husband absolutely loves this stew. It is a lot of work, due to all of the chopping, but he deserves it! He refers to it as the "full treatment" since I include every vegetable in the produce aisle that looks good (be creative). It is filling, yet light and healthy; and even more delectable the next day. The vegetables and wine result in a richly flavored stock; thus either broth or water may be used to lighten the soup and increase the yield.

Stew Meat

Star Anise Perfumed Venison in a Potato Kale Stew

Slow Cooker

For the Venison
- stew meat, 1.5 lbs, 2" cubes
- 2 Tbs olive oil
- 1 Tbs sea salt
- 30 grinds of black pepper

For the Vegetable Sauté
- 2 Tbs olive oil
- 10 garlic cloves, minced
- 2 tsp sea salt
- 2 russet potatoes, 1" cubes
- 2 stalks of celery, sliced
- 8 carrots, sliced

For the Final Crock Pot Additions
- 1 head of green chard, chopped
- 2 tsp sea salt
- ⅓ cup of favorite red wine
- 8 cups of beef broth
- 4 cups water
- 2 star anise pods
- 1 Tbs ancho chili pepper
- 1 Tbs ground cardamom

Details: (if your crock pot insert is not stove top safe, use a sauté pan)
- Coat the rump roast with salt and pepper
- Heat olive oil in a stovetop safe, crock pot insert (or sauté pan) over high heat until shimmering; sear the venison on all sides until browned; transfer to a plate
- Add all of the Vegetable Sauté ingredients to the crock pot; sauté for ~ 5 min
- Add the chard and 2 tsp salt; sauté for another 2 min; transfer the insert to the crock pot; top with the wine, broth, water, star anise, chili powder, and cardamom
- Cover and slow cook the stew on High Power for ~ 6 – 8 hr and serve

NOTE:

Star anise is a dried spice obtained from Chinese evergreen trees that looks like a star and tastes like anise. The flavor of star anise pods is akin to fennel or savory liquorice, and lends an intoxicatingly unique aroma and flavor here. It is often used in baking, and along with fennel, in the production of absinthe. It is also used as an herbal remedy to treat rheumatism and aid in digestion.

Grinding Venison

GROUND VENISON

NOTE: Grinding venison can be done easily at home with a meat grinder or mixer attachment (both appliances are shown at left). Weigh the venison and add ~ 1 – 10 % fat, by weight, if desired. Note that bacon or beef fat with sinew attached can clog the grinder. Trim fat of sinew, etc. prior to adding to the grinder, or use lard.

Venison Cali Burgers

For the Venison Burgers (mix together by hand to form three ⅓ lb patties)
- ground venison, ~ 1 lb
- ¼ cup favorite steak sauce

Burger Assembly Accouterments
- avocado slices
- tomato slices
- buffalo wing sauce
- green leafy lettuce
- bleu or jack cheese, *optional*
- whole grain rolls (page 168)

Details: Preheat grill with a med-high flame
- Form 3 or 4 burger patties; grill for ~ 4 - 5 min on each side to medium doneness; toast the buns lightly on the grill ~ 20 sec; assemble burgers with accouterments

NOTE: Buffalo wing sauce is without question my favorite condiment. It is especially good here paired with creamy avocado, making the blue or pepper jack cheese optional.

Classic Venison Tacos

For the Venison Tacos

- ground venison, ~ 1 lb
- ⅔ cup water

- 1 package of taco seasoning, or ⅓ cup desired taco spices

Taco Assembly Accouterments

- grated cheddar cheese
- sour cream
- iceberg lettuce, chopped

- tomatoes, diced
- favorite hot sauce, or salsa
- 6 hard taco shells

Details: Preheat oven to 350 °F (bake)

- Brown venison in a sauté pan over high heat, ~ 4 min; add the taco seasoning
- Reduce heat to med; stir in water ~2 min until thickened; remove pan from heat
- Bake the taco shells ~ 6 min to crisp; remove from oven; assemble the tacos

Ground Venison

Venison Bolognese

Venison Meat Sauce, Sauté and Stovetop Simmer

For the Venison Sauté
- ground venison, ~1.25 lbs
- 9 garlic cloves + 1 tsp salt
- 1 Tbs fennel seeds
- 4 Tbs olive oil

- 2 tsp red pepper flakes
- 2 tsp sea salt
- 20 grinds pepper
- ⅓ cup white wine, to deglaze

For the Simmer Ingredients
- 1 Tbs capers + 1 Tbs salt
- 28 oz can crushed tomatoes

- 28 oz can whole tomatoes, slightly pureed, or left whole

For the Grand Finale
- 0.66 oz pack fresh basil, extra leaves for garnish

- Parmigiano Reggiano cheese, grated

Details: see Lessons on deglazing, page 253
- Roughly mince the garlic; top with 1 tsp salt and fennel seeds; finely mince this blend; garlic sticks to the fennel seeds, preventing them from flying everywhere
- Heat 4 Tbs olive oil in a stock pot over high heat until shimmering; add the red pepper flakes and minced garlic-fennel to the oil; sauté ~ 45 sec (do not burn)
- Add the ground venison, 2 tsp salt, and pepper; brown the venison until the pink just disappears while breaking apart clumps; add the wine to deglaze for ~ 30 sec
- Reduce heat to low; add all Simmer Ingredients; stir, cover, and simmer for ~ 1 hr
- Chiffonade the basil leaves; stack and roll them into a ball; cut into thin strips
- Remove the lid; add the basil; stir and simmer uncovered, or partially covered, to thicken the sauce to your desired consistency while preparing whole wheat pasta
- Serve with basil leaves and grated Parmigiano over whole wheat pasta (page 178)

NOTE: After 15 years of making Bolognese sauce, this version is our favorite. Slightly pureeing the second can of whole tomatoes yields a juicier sauce, with a more interesting and controlled texture. For canned whole tomatoes, San Marzanos are best. They are sweet, tart, vibrant, and have few seeds. Substitute 2 Tbs sugar for the wine if desired.

VENISON JERKY

Venison Jerky Three Ways

3 Awesome Marinades for Addictive Venison Jerky
- Venison, flank is best, trim all fat, ~ 1.5 lbs per ~ ¾ cup of marinade

Chipotle Lime	Jalapeño Lemon	Ginger Scallion
1 Tbs salt	1 Tbs salt	1 Tbs salt
30 grinds black pepper	30 grinds black pepper	3 scallions minced
2 garlic cloves, minced	2 garlic cloves, minced	1 garlic clove, minced
2 Tbs sherry vinegar	2 Tbs white wine vinegar	1 Tbs ginger, grated
3 Tbs chipotle flakes	3 Tbs jalapeño flakes	1 Tbs red pepper flakes
3 Tbs Worcestershire sauce	3 Tbs soy sauce	3 Tbs rice wine vinegar
juice of 1 lime	juice of 1 lemon	1 Tbs soy sauce

Details: If you do not own a dehydrator (no problem, it is not needed), preheat oven to 160 °F (dehydrate convection) or your lowest oven temperature (bake), ~ 180 °F

- Partially dethaw venison; trim all fat to prevent the jerky from going rancid; cut ⅛" slices along the grain or against the grain; semi-frozen meat allows for precision
- Whisk chosen marinade ingredients together in a medium bowl; add ~1.5 lb sliced venison; cover and marinate overnight in the fridge; remove from the fridge the following day and keep covered at room temp until you are ready to dehydrate
- Pour off excess liquid; then gently squeeze excess liquid out of the venison
- Lay the venison strips in between paper towels to extract more of the marinade; the goal is to dehydrate; thus removing excess liquid reduces the oven drying time
- Transfer the venison slices onto a nonstick or stainless steel rack positioned over a rimmed pan, as shown in the photos at left
- Dehydrate for 1 hr at 160 °F; reduce to 140 °F; continue drying for ~ 2 – 3 hr
  - Or, dehydrate at 180 °F for ~ 2½ – 3 hr total

NOTE: Many recipes note that cutting against the grain will result in a more tender jerky. As long as you do not over dry the meat or cut it too thin, cutting it with the grain results in an appealing bite. Jerky cut against the grain may be easier for some to chew, although will crumble if over-dried. Test for dryness and doneness by flexing the meat. It may also be noted that the FDA recommends a temp of 160 °F to kill bacteria, though you may choose to dehydrate at 140 °F the entire time for ~ 3 – 4 hr total.

So God created human beings in his image. God blessed them… God said, "Look, I **have given you all the plants that have grain** for seeds and all the trees whose fruits have seeds in them. They will be food for you." And it happened. **God looked at everything he had made, and it was very good**. This was the sixth day.

~ **Genesis 1: 27, 28, 29, 30, 31 NCV**

Chris was traveling, and texted me to see how I was doing; so I asked a stranger to snap this photo for him. I was dispensing honey in the whole grains food section having the time of my life. I didn't know it at the time, but my cart was full of ~ **Deuteronomy 8:8**, **A land of wheat, and barley, and vines, and fig trees, and pomegranates; a land of oil olive, and honey…** ~ KJV

Chapter 2: For the GRAINIACS

- Whole Grain Storage
- Types of Gluten Containing & Gluten-Free Grains and Pseudo-Grains
- Whole Grains Cooking Methods and Time Table
  - WHEAT FAMILY
    - Wheat Berry and Balsamic Broccoli Red Pepper Salad
    - Spelt Berries with Artichokes, Green Pepper, and Lemon Feta Salad
    - Kamut with Lemon, Parsley, and Cherry Tomatoes
    - Tarragon Leek Tabbouleh
    - Farro with Roasted Red Pepper, Kalamata Olives, and Goat Cheese
  - RYE BERRIES
    - Rye Berry Salad of Carrots, Radicchio, and Radishes
  - BARLEY
    - Barley with Greek Yogurt and Honey
  - OAT GROATS
    - Breakfast Blends for a Week
  - BROWN RICE
    - Perfect Brown Rice & Brown Sugar Rice Pudding
    - Ginger Perfumed Sweet Brown Sushi Rice
    - Romantic Rice ~ Red, Forbidden, and Jasmine
    - Wild Rice and Brown Basmati Blend
  - QUINOA
    - Greenwa Quinoa Cilantro Lime Serrano Salad
  - MILLET
    - Millet Pilaf with Heirloom Tomatoes and Dilled Sweet Corn
  - BUCKWHEAT
    - Buckwheat with Cremini Mushrooms, Roasted Garlic & Micro Greens
  - AMARANTH
    - Amaranth Polenta with Sugar Peas, Shitakes, & Sun-Dried Tomatoes
  - TEFF
    - Teff Caprese Tart with Beefsteak Vinegar and Tomatoes
  - CORN
    - Jalapeño Smoked Cheddar Blue and Yellow Corn Grits

Whole Grain Storage

Achieve Inner Peace through Organization in Every Aspect of your Life

A healthy obsession with grains is just that – healthy. Store grains out of the heat, light, and air with labels on Ziploc bags or plastic containers.

Joseph knew that Grain Storage could mean Life or Death

Joseph said, "Listen to the dream I had. We were in the field tying bundles of wheat together. My bundle stood up, and your bundles of wheat gathered around it and bowed down to it." His brothers said, "Do you really think you will be king over us? His brothers hated him even more because of his dreams and what he had said.

~ Genesis 37: 6, 7, 8 NCV

Two years later the king dreamed he was standing on the bank of the Nile River. The next morning the king was troubled about these dreams, so he sent for all the magicians and wise men of Egypt. The king told them his dreams, but no one could explain their meaning to him. So the king called for Joseph. The guards quickly brought him out of the prison, and he shaved, put on clean clothes, and went before the king. The king said to Joseph "... I saw seven full and good heads of grain growing on one stalk. Then Joseph said to the king, "God is telling you what he is about to do. ...the seven thin heads of grain burned by the hot east wind stand for seven years of hunger. So let the king choose a man who is very wise and understanding and set him over the land of Egypt. And let the king also appoint officers over the land, who should take one-fifth of all the food that is grown during the seven good years. That food should be saved to use during the seven years of hunger that will come on the land of Egypt. Then the people in Egypt will not die during the seven years of hunger." The hunger was everywhere in that part of the world. And Joseph opened the storehouses and sold grain to the people of Egypt, because the time of hunger became terrible in Egypt.

~ Genesis 41: 1, 8, 14, 15, 22, 25, 27, 33-36 NCV

Jacob learned that there was grain in Egypt, so he said to his sons, "Why are you just sitting here looking at one another? Go down there and buy grain for us to eat, so that we will live and not die." ten of Joseph's brothers went down to buy grain from Egypt. Now Joseph was governor over Egypt.
He was the one who sold the grain to people who came to buy it.
So Joseph's brothers came to him and bowed facedown on the ground before him. Joseph knew they were his brothers, but they did not know who he was.

~ Genesis 42: 1, 2, 3, 6, 8 NCV

Read Genesis to learn more about Joseph's Incredible Life

Whole Grains that Contain Gluten

Hard Red Wheat   Soft White Wheat   Spelt

Coarse Bulgur   Kamut   Farro   Light Bulgur

Rye   Barley   Triticale

Whole Grains that Contain Gluten

1. HARD RED WHEAT BERRIES –

Hard red wheat berries are small, short, oblong kernels with a red-hued tan color sold as either winter or spring wheat, indicating their planting season. Wheat is often referred to as the "staff of life" as this nutrient dense grain contains vitamins (Bs and E), minerals, niacin, iron, magnesium, folacin, zinc, pantothenic acid, thiamin, chromium, and manganese. Vitamin E is a powerful antioxidant; and in wheat, it slows the germs' oils from going rancid when milled.

Einkorn is the oldest strain of wheat dating back to 10,000 B.C. These amber waves of grain have covered much of North America since the 17th century, although it was the Egyptians who discovered that wheat's **gluten** could produce leavened bread. Gluten is the elastic protein responsible for the stretch in your dough. Hard wheat is known for its high protein content, starting at ~ 10.5 % for winter wheat, and increases to ~ 17 % for spring. Increased protein results in lighter loaves (think spring wheat, springier). Wheat berries contain 4 types of protein: gliadin, glutenin, albumin, and globulin (the latter two are water-soluble). Note that wheat kernels alone do not contain gluten. It isn't formed until the two water insoluble proteins, gliadin and glutenin, are hydrated and react to form the colloidal (water insoluble) polymer we know as gluten. Specifically, glutenin is the long chain polymer responsible for the dough's stretch. Gliadin is the crosslinking agent that bonds glutenin chains together to form 3-dimensinoals networks, giving the dough its strength (for you polymer chemists). The amount of gliadin dictates the length that dough can extend before it will break (the maximum % elongation). Hard wheat is ground for commercial all-purpose baking flour (whole wheat or white), and hard spring wheat is especially good for the high loft popovers featured in this book.

2. SOFT WHITE WHEAT BERRIES –

Soft white wheat berries are similar in size to hard red wheat; although slightly rounder, and light tan in color. They too, can be planted in either winter or spring. The main difference in soft wheat is that it has a lower protein content, typically ranging from ~ 6 - 10 %. The lower protein and analogous gluten content, makes soft wheat the choice of bakers for cakes and muffins where a tender crumb is preferred over springy bread. If you grind your own grains, use soft wheat to mill fresh, nutritious pastry flour for baked goods. If purchasing, look for ground soft white wheat, labeled as either "cake" or "pastry flour". Soft white wheat offers a similar nutritional profile to that of hard wheat, though with a slightly higher fiber content of 6 g / ¼ cup relative to 5 g / ¼ cup for red (amounts vary per source; Bob's Red Mill fiber values are given herein). Hard white winter wheat berries are a relatively new strain with a similar protein profile to that of hard winter red, though lighter in color and potentially more appealing to the public.

3. SPELT –

Spelt was gathered as far back as 6000 B.C. In fact, einkorn, emmer, and spelt were responsible for ending the nomadic, food-gathering lifestyle in the New Stone Age era. Once people stopped searching for random patches of wheat and learned to sow, grow, and harvest it, wheat became a commodity and communities were established. Ancient spelt is a crossbreed of emmer. It has an orange-tan hue and is slightly larger than wheat. Spelt has a slightly sweeter wheat taste than other grains within the wheat family.

Interestingly, many people with wheat sensitivities or celiac disease can often tolerate spelt because it contains a distinct protein profile. It is thought that spelt contains a different form of gliadin, which is the protein that those with wheat allergies cannot digest. It contains more protein than hard wheat, though yields less gluten. Spelt's high protein content results in quick rising dough, though fragile, due to its dissimilar gliadin quality. Thus, spelt cannot form breads with as much spring as traditional wheat breads, which get their loft from 3-D networks that are strong enough to entrain plenty of air without rupturing throughout the kneading, rising, and baking processes.

4. COARSE BULGUR –

Bulgur, also referred to as burghul, is a form of processed wheat. While processed, it is still considered a whole grain as it contains the germ, bran, and endosperm. It is partially steamed, dried, and cracked into smaller pieces or left whole. This pre-cooking method allows bulgur to be prepared for cereals, salads, or pilafs in about half the time as that for whole wheat berries. Red or white wheat can be used to produce bulgur, and the size of the grind dictates its cooking time. Look for grinds such as: coarse (#4 or #3), medium (#2), or fine (#1). Grinds 1 through 3 often do not require boiling on the stovetop, but rather a soak in boiling water on the countertop; making it a rapid, yet nutritious, alternative to traditional wheat berries. Bulgur's nutritional profile is similar to that of its parent grain. This "fast food" processed alternative to wheat berries originated in the Middle East and is also a staple food in North Africa and the Balkans. Coarse bulgur is featured here in a non-traditional Middle Eastern Tabbouleh salad with a twist. When using bulgur in pilafs or salads, test the doneness prior to incorporating the remaining ingredients. The age of the grain still dictates cooking time.

5. LIGHT BULGAR –

Light bulgur is prepared from soft or hard white wheat kernels, rather than red. It is also available in a variety of grind sizes allowing for a myriad of fluffy to dense textures. Grinds #1 and #2 resemble wheat germ and grits, respectively. When fully cooked, fine and medium bulgur resembles cous cous. As light bulgur is prepared from white wheat, it has a slightly higher fiber content relative to red wheat based bulgur. Both red and white bulgur, have slightly less fiber than the parent berry as some of the bran is lost during the processing method; although it still contains roughly twice as much fiber than rice. In addition to use in pilafs and Tabbouleh salads, bulgur is an effective thickening agent when added to soups and stews. Add it to jambalaya rather than rice to break tradition. You might also try adding it to the grain soaks noted in some of the whole grain breads featured herein for extra fiber, texture, or even a hint of crunch (with less soaking).

6. KAMUT® –

Kamut, is golden bronze in color, long, and slender; and it is the largest grain in the wheat family. It is a registered trademark originally coined by wheat farmers, Bob Quinn and his son T. Mack, of Montana. The trademark ensures that the grain is organically grown. The name Kamut means "soul of the earth" and refers to its folklore history. In 1977, the Quinns purchased a jar containing 36 grains from a U.S. airman who claimed to have recovered them from a box found near an Egyptian tomb. While the grains were not actually harvested from King Tut's tomb, it was cultivated in Egypt, and it is a current relative of durum wheat. Again, some with wheat allergies may be able to tolerate Kamut. It contains more vitamin E than wheat; and like spelt, has a sweeter taste, higher protein content, and a different quality of gliadin relative to wheat. Recall network quality and strength regarding bread making. In addition to the types of proteins available in wheat, their network forming ability also relies on the ground bran fraction and size. Bran is the reason that whole wheat flour does not produce the same loft as white flour based breads. Sharply edged bran pieces cut into and break the polymer strands connecting the network. Since Kamut has a thinner bran layer than hard wheat berries, it is capable of producing loaves with a similar spring. When cooked, these substantial plump grains pair beautifully with juicy vegetables such as cherry tomatoes.

7. FARRO -

Farro is the Italian translation of the English word 'emmer'. Farro grains have a distinctly beautiful matte finish due to the pearling process that the emmer wheat undergoes. The level of pearling dictates the color. White farro, or 'perlato', has little bran, whereas tan and tan speckled, or 'semi-perlato' farro, retains more of its bran. Farro is a relatively new and trendy grain, being served in the most stylish Italian restaurants and worldwide. Its popularity is easily understood due to its distinctly pleasing chew from its thinner bran layer. Farro does not harden when refrigerated, and it cooks relatively fast in comparison to wheat, spelt, Kamut, and triticale, each of which has all of their bran intact. Like spelt and Kamut, some people with wheat allergies can also tolerate farro.

8. BARLEY -

Barley, possibly the oldest cultivated cereal, dates as far back as wheat to 10,000 B.C., as evidenced in Syria. Today, barley follows after wheat, rice, and corn as the world's fourth largest cereal crop. This light tan, short, plump grain has a nutritional profile similar to wheat; and is high in essential minerals, tryptophan and selenium. It has the highest amount of fiber (9 g / ¼ cup) of the grains with gluten; and includes beta-glucan, the heart healthy, soluble fiber, which is known to reduce cholesterol. Barley stews, cereals, and risottos are nutty in flavor and buttery in texture, thanks to its high amylopectin content, a sticky starch that gives way to a viscous, glossy sheen. When sprouted, barley is high in maltose, which is used to make malt syrup, or fermented to produce beer. With regard to nutrition, it is worthwhile to understand barley's terminology. Barley kernels are encased in two layers of an inedible hull. "Hulled" barley requires an abrasion process, called hulling, to remove the tightly bound hull, which also removes some of the bran. Note that the bran contains the majority of the grain's fiber, protein, and B vitamins. "Hull-less" barley is a new variety in which the hulls naturally fall off during harvesting, thus no pearling is needed. Most barley found in the supermarket is white in color and labeled as "pearled", where the germ and most of the fiber have been removed. Since barley's fiber is dispersed throughout the grain as well as the bran, cooked pearled barley still contains twice as much fiber as brown rice.

9. RYE BERRIES –

Rye berries are long, lean, and green. These gorgeous high-fiber khaki-hued grains contain more iron, protein, phosphorus, potassium, B vitamins, magnesium, calcium, lignans, antioxidants, and lysine than wheat. While high in protein, rye does not form glutinous, elastic dough. Rather, it forms gummy, sticky dough due to it high level of hydrophilic (water loving) pentosans, which are fragile polysaccharides responsible for the moist, dense, texture of pumpernickel breads. Rye is also high in amylase enzymes, which convert starches to sugars (which further weakens dough's network); thus a sourdough starter is often used to slow the amylase activity. This robust grain can survive almost anywhere, even in subzero climates, and has a rich European history, particularly in Russia. While hardy, rye it is susceptible to ergot, a fungus that can cause hallucinations and death. It was thought to be partially responsible for the Salem witchcraft episodes. In this book, an easy to handle rye dough is featured in crackers complimented with caraway seeds.

10. TRITICALE –

Triticale is a rye-wheat hybrid. Its name is derived from the Latin words for wheat (Triticum) and rye (Secale). This pudgy grain has a tan-khaki hue, and a slightly wrinkled bran. It was first produced in 1888 and contains twice the lysine of wheat and more protein than wheat and rye (up to 17%). It is excellent for the liver and removes plaques from the body.

Gluten-Free Whole Grains

Oat Groats Brown Rice Wild Rice

Quinoa Millet Buckwheat Amaranth

Teff Corn Sorghum

Gluten-Free Whole Grains & Pseudo-Grains

The Following Grains are Gluten-Free when Pure - Not Crossbred or Contaminated

The gluten-free grains that follow cannot be made to into baked goods with a springy texture on their own, although they can be combined with wheat flours to infuse interesting textures and an abundance of nutrients within breads and beyond.

1.   OAT GROATS – Gluten-Free

Oat groats are the slender, tan grain with a beautiful matte finish and soft bran layer that we have all come to know and love as various forms of oatmeal. You may be familiar with instant oats (thin flakes), old-fashioned or thick rolled oats (rolled from whole groats), and steel-cut, Scotch, or Irish oats (whole groats cut into bits with a steel blade). Though, if you have not yet tried cooked whole oat groats, you are in for a treat. Oats are high in polyphenols and famous for their high levels of both soluble fiber (lowers blood cholesterol) and insoluble fiber (promotes digestive regularity). It is this soluble fiber, the beta-glucans, which gives oat groats their buttery smooth, yet chewy texture and a similar glossy sheen to that of barley when cooked. Oats contain B vitamins and are higher in protein and Fe than wheat. High in nutrition, thankfully the Scottish helped remove the class stigma from oats after 19th century French and English knights refused to eat *animal feed and peasant food.* The English dictionary of Samuel Johnson defined oats as "food for men in Scotland, horses in England". The Scots rebutted with, "England is noted for the excellence of her horses: Scotland for the excellence of her men". Oats are featured herein as sweet, creamy, hearty breakfast meals and in whole grain breads.

2.   BROWN RICE – Gluten-Free

Whole grain rice exudes the color of its bran. In this book, several types of brown, black, and red are introduced as main or side dishes. Brown rice is an excellent source of manganese and a good source of selenium and magnesium. Second in production to wheat, nearly 2 billion people consume rice as 25 - 50 % of their diet. This is likely because rice is one of the most easily digested proteins, and it is particularly valuable as a complex carbohydrate.

Whole grain brown rice (complete with its bran, endosperm, and germ) is digested more slowly than white rice and therefore has a lower glycemic index. Polished white rice has significantly less nutritional value, as its germ and brand have been removed. Whole grain rice is cultivated in short, medium, and long lengths. All rice contains two types of starch: amylose (non-sticky) and amylopectin (sticky). Shorter grains have higher percentages of amylopectin, yielding sticky rice dishes, opposed to long grain, fluffy finished dishes. Since there are 1000s of varieties and forms of rice available today, they can be used in anything from sweet morning cereals, to sticky sushi rice and molds, as well as light pilaf vegetable blends. In addition to varied textures, aromatic rices exude a nutty aroma during cooking; look for jasmine, basmati, and kalijira. The varied hues and finishes also add excitement to dishes over standard, pearled white rice.

3. WILD RICE – Gluten-Free

Wild rice is not actually a grain or a grass, but rather a pseudo-grain. Pseudo-grains are typically seeds that are similar in appearance to whole grains and are cooked in the same manner. Pseudo-grains are commonly accepted as whole grains due to their similar or enhanced nutritional profiles. Wild rice is the seed of an aquatic grass. North American wild rice originated in the Great Lake regions of Minnesota, and is also grown in Wisconsin, Michigan, Canada, California, and Oregon. Though lower in minerals than rice, wild rice is much higher in protein, fiber, and high in B vitamins. These long, slender, dark mahogany hued seeds ablaze with flecks of bronze and gold are visually stunning. Wild rice goes through a 4-stage process prior to distribution, which includes: drying, parching, hulling, and winnowing to remove the hulls from the edible grain. As with other grains, darker colored seeds indicate that more bran has been left in tact; and require slightly longer cooking times. When cooked, it unfurls slightly to yield a thirst quenching, center ready to soak up any nearby gourmet sauce. With its exotic nutty flavor and tea-like aroma, it is also delicious on its own, or blended with other grains. Truly wild, hand collected grains are expensive relative to those cultivated on a commercial scale. The length of the seed also dictates the cost, with the longest commanding the highest prices (up to 1", called "giant" and ½" called "extra fancy"). Blending grains with wild rice is a great way to enjoy this luxurious grain, while saving on cost. In this book, it is paired with long grain basmati brown rice as an elegant side dish to soak up wild game, deglazed, wine au jus and a hint of lemon pepper juice from the roasted squash.

4. QUINOA – Gluten-Free

Quinoa, rhymes with green-wa, and is the basis of my favorite recipe in this book (a lime, cilantro, pepper and avocado salad). Not a grain, but rather a pseudo-grain; these seeds originate from a vegetable of the broad-leaved goosefoot family (related to Swiss chard and beets). Quinoa originated high in the South American Andes and was dubbed the sacred "mother grain" by ancient Incas. It is harvested in a variety of hues: black, red, pink, purple, and orange; though pale gold, ivory are the most abundant. These tiny disc-shaped seeds, with the cute little indents, are protein powerhouses (up to ~ 20 %) as the germ makes up about 60 % of the grain. They are a complete protein since they contain all of the essential amino acids, including lysine, methionine, and cystine. It is also high in fiber, iron, calcium, magnesium, phosphorus, and B vitamins and vitamin E. Their unique extra-terrestrial like shape leads to an equally extra-ordinary texture. When cooked, the concentric band unfurls and leaves its mother ship. The result is a pleasing blend of semi-crunchy "tails" that compliment the host's silken-soft, bouncy, center "beads". Quinoa is harvested with a thin layer of saponins, a bitter tasting alkaloid (a natural, soapy, insect repellant), which should be rinsed off prior to cooking unless its label states that it has been prewashed (such as those from Bob's Red Mill).

5. MILLET – Gluten-Free

Millet, dating back to 7000 BC, is deemed one of China's 5 sacred crops (along with rice, barley, soya, and wheat), and is a staple food in Africa today. These tiny little grains look similar to quinoa in bulk, although upon closer inspection, they are more yellow in color and have a much rounder shape. Millet has a delicious nutty sweetness, similar to that of sweet corn; and has a uniquely, crunchy yet tender, texture combination. Previously known for its use in birdseed, it is thankfully making a culinary comeback with style. Hulling does not affect millet's impressive nutritional profile as the germ is contained within the grain. Millet is very high in fiber (9 g / ¼ cup), magnesium, antioxidants, and also high in iron, phytic acid, protein (~ 15%), lysine, methionine, B vitamins, vitamin E, potassium, phosphorus, copper, and manganese. Finger millet, one of 12 species, is very high in calcium. Like rice, millet is also easy to digest and nonallergenic. Herein, it lends a fantastic crunch to whole grain breads, and is paired as a pilaf with sweet corn, fresh dill, and tomatoes.

6. BUCKWHEAT – Gluten-Free

Originating out of southwest Asia's mountains back in 4000 BC, buckwheat is not a form of wheat; nor is it a grain. This pseudo-grain is a flowering plant seed related to rhubarb and sorrel in the Polygonaceae family. Orchard bees are attracted to the pink and white flowers, gifting us with a dark, distinctly flavored honey. These cute little heart-shaped pyramidal grains offer a uniquely earthy taste and equally singular toothsome bite. Though darling, it is also hardy and thrives in the Arctic and Himalayas. Buckwheat contains 8 essential amino acids; and it is high in zinc, copper, manganese, magnesium, B vitamins, iron, phosphorus, potassium, vitamin E, and calcium. It is the only grain known to have high levels of rutin, an antioxidant shown to improve circulation, control high blood pressure, and lower LDL cholesterol. Ground buckwheat flour is notable in Japanese soba noodles, caviar topped Russian blinis, American pancakes, and French galettes. Whole roasted buckwheat groats (darker in color) may be best known in the Russian dish, kasha. Roasted buckwheat groats are toasted and commonly sold as "kasha". Purchase kasha in a store with good turnover as older roasted groats can go rancid. In this book, unroasted buckwheat groats are featured in an Asian fusion salad.

7. AMARANTH – Gluten-Free

Amaranth is not a grain, but rather the seed of a beautiful annual herb with red-crimson flowers. Its name is derived from the Greek word for immortal. Amaranth was a staple of Aztec culture until Cortez, in an effort to destroy that civilization, decreed that anyone growing the crop would be put to death. Seeds were smuggled out to Asia, where locals referred to amaranth as the "seed sent by God" as a tribute to its taste and sustenance. Though not the tiniest pseudo-grain (teff is), I might argue it as the cutest. Check out the equatorial Saturn-band (its germ) that encompasses the pudgy shaped center, similar to quinoa, but without the central indent. A cousin of quinoa, amaranth has the highest content of protein of all grains, especially lysine. This superpower grain is also high in fiber, calcium, phosphorus, iron, and vitamins C, B, and E. It is typically harvested in ebony or beige hues. Cooked amaranth resembles brown caviar and has a uniquely silken texture due to its high amylopectin content. It also has a pleasing slight after-crunch. In Mexico, it is popped like popcorn, mixed with syrup, and sold on the streets as "alegria".

8. TEFF - Gluten-Free

Teff, the tiniest pseudo-grain, is a member of the genus Eragrostis (lovegrass). This minuscule Ethiopian seed is most commonly used as ground flour to produce Ethiopia's national bread, injera, a flat bread that doubles as an edible plate for stews. Naturally sweet in flavor, and loaded with calcium, iron, phosphorus, copper, and fiber, teff serves as a highly nutritious porridge similar in texture to farina. In fact, teff has more calcium than any grain (123 mg / cup), is high in Vitamin C, and is a complete protein with all 8 essential amino acids. Here, I use teff as a firm polenta tart for a tangy Caprese salad.

9. CORN - Gluten-Free

Corn is best known as sweet kernels on the cob, but not necessarily as a gluten-free, whole grain. There are 5 major types of dried corn: dent or field (for grits), flint (for johnnycakes, hominy, and masa harina), popcorn (has a high moisture content), and flour (for tortillas, chips, and quick breads). The sweet kernels (maize) are delicious cooked alone, in baked goods, salads, chilies, grits, and polentas. High in natural starch sugars, it is a common source of fructose. Most cornmeal is "degerminated", thus not a whole grain; so look for sources that include brown flecks of germ and refrigerate it. Corn offers more antioxidants than any other grains, and 10 times the amount of vitamin A. It is also high in fiber, thiamin, pantothenic acid, folate, vitamin C, phosphorus, and manganese. When consumed with beans or meat, its amino acid profile forms a complete protein.

10. SORGHUM – Gluten-Free

Sorghum is a plump, medium sized, oval grain, pale golden in color with beautiful pinkish-coral undertones. Also called milo or kafir; it is a staple grain of Africa, Asia, and India, and is a good source of antioxidants, protein, phosphorus, and potassium. The juice in the stalks is used as sorghum syrup and molasses. As the cooked whole grain can be dry and mealy chilled, it is delicious warm. Milled, it is a sweet tasting, gluten-free flour perfect for moist baked goods. Milled sorghum is used here as a complementary flour to 100% dark cocoa to enhance the sweetness and density of intensely rich Chocolate Poeuffs.

Whole Grain Cooking Methods

Again Jesus began to teach by the lake. He told them, "The secret to the kingdom of God has been given to you. The farmer sows the word. Some people are like seed along the path, where the word is sown." He also said, "This is what the kingdom of God is like. A man scatters seed on the ground. Night and day, whether he sleeps or gets up, the seed sprouts and grows, though he does not know how. All by itself the soil produces grain – first the stalk, then the head, then the full kernel in the head. As soon as the grain is ripe, he puts the sickle to it, because the harvest has come."

~ Mark 4:1, 11, 14, 15, 26-29 NIV

Verily, verily, I say unto you, Except a corn of wheat fall into the ground and die, it abideth alone: but if it die, if bringeth forth much fruit. He that loveth his life shall lose it, and he that hateth his life in this world shall keep it unto life eternal.

~ John 12: 24-25 KJV

Whole Grains Die When Cooked and Revitalize you Upon Consumption:

- Use the Whole Grains Cooking Time Table on the next page, and the guidelines below, on method and water to perfect your favorite technique for each grain

Cooking Method (Time):

- Stovetop Simmer – slowest method - offers the most control as you can simply lift the lid to check on doneness and adjust the heat on the stovetop
- Pressure Cooker – fastest method - offers least control as depressurizing is required to check doneness, and re-pressurizing may be necessary
- Rice Cooker – a simple method - experimentation may be necessary as different manufacturers offer different rice functions based on water sorption and time
- Toasting – few minute dry sauté prior to cooking in water - brings out the flavor and minimizes clumping in smaller grains such as millet, teff, and buckwheat

Amount of Water (Texture):

- You can relate this concept to cooking instant oatmeal, soupy versus firm
- Less water can yield individual grains perfect for hearty chewy breakfast cereals, salads, pilafs, or firm polentas
- More water with starch results in porridges, risottos, soups, or soft polentas

Whole Grains Cooking Time Table

The texture of whole grains is considered best when cooked like pasta (al dente), rather than water logged; though your appliance and taste may garner longer cooking times. Older dried grains (several years) or beans will require longer cooking times. It is typically best to err on less time initially, and increase as needed. My preferred minimum cooking times follow; and I encourage experimentation to find your own.

Whole Grain 1 cup Dried Grain	Stovetop Simmer		Pressure Cooker		Rice Cooker	Approximate Cooked Yield	Nutrition per ¼ cup Uncooked Whole Grain			
	Water	Time	Water	Time (min)	Function	cups	Fiber (g)	Protein (g)	Ca (%)	Fe (%)
Wheat Berries	3	1 hour	1 ¾	35	brown	3	6	6	2	8
Spelt	2	25 min	1 ¾	15	brown	3	4	6	0	10
Farro	2	25 min	1 ¾	15	brown	3	4	6	2	6
Kamut	3	1 hour 15 min	1 ¾	40	brown	3	4	7	2	10
Coarse Bulgur*	1 ½	10 min	1 ½	5	white	2 ½	7	5	2	6
Light Bulgur*	1 ½	10 min	1 ½	5	white	2 ½	4	4	0	6
Rye Berries	3	50 min	1 ¾	25	brown	3	6	6	2	10
Triticale	3	1 hour	1 ¾	30	brown	3	7	6	2	6
Barley	3 ½	1 hour 30 min	1 ¾	50	brown	3	8	6	2	10
Oat Groats	3	1 hour	1 ¾	35	brown	3	5	6	2	10
Brown Rice	2	40 min	1 ½	15	brown	3	3	3	0	2
Wild Rice	2	45 min	1 ½	15	brown	3	2	4	0	4
Quinoa	1 ¾	13 min	1 ¾	6	white	3	3	7	2	10
Millet**	2	15 min	1 ¾	8	white	3	9	7	0	8
Buckwheat***	1 ¾	10 min	1 ¾	5	white	3	5	6	0	6
Amaranth**	1 ½	20 min	1 ½	10	white	2 ½	7	8	8	20
Teff**	3	25 min	1 ¾	5	white	3 ½	4	7	10	20
Sorghum	3	55 min	1 ¾	30	brown	2 ½	8	5	0	8
Cornmeal	4	40 min	2 ½	20	brown	3	5	2	1	6

Note - always add ~ 1 Tbs of oil or butter per cup of grain for pressure cooking

* no simmering necessary; rather let stand covered with boiling water for 45 min - 1 hr

** toast in a dry skillet over med-high heat for ~ 4 min

*** saute to coat with an egg or egg white for ~ 4 min

Macrobiotics, Grains & Sea Vegetables

During my first and only visit with the hospital's dietician, we discussed my doctor's diagnosis and possible remedies. After reviewing the myriad of prescriptions I tried over the years to no avail for a semi-paralyzed lower GI tract, she was unsure whether any dietary change would help. Initially, when doctors told me to "eat more fiber", I sought high fiber breakfast cereals and aimed to eat an apple a day. This was ineffective, as I would toss the grainy apples, and most of the 'whole grain' cereals I chose were highly processed. I detailed my aversion to fruit, based on countless experiences with bruised, soft-mushy-mealy spots, hard or under-ripe segments, and often-tasteless commercial produce. I didn't have the funds or desire to waste food; so, with the exception of citrus fruits, I stopped trying fruit altogether. I also explained that the next step in my treatment was a colectomy; so I was willing to follow *any* recommendations she had.

She took the approach of treating my system like a newborn's, and instructed me to begin an elimination diet; which involves the isolation and systematic re-introduction of new foods, to gage the body's response. Considering celiac disease as one potential malady, she suggested an exclusive diet of brown rice as an initial, conceivable remedy. Brown rice is gluten free, easy to digest, and a great introduction to the world of unprocessed, whole grains. It is also the basis of many well-balanced macrobiotic diets.

I later learned in our appointment that macrobiotics is not only a diet, but also a way of life; and that whole grains are *the* principal food within this philosophy. So – it was out with the white, pearled, and processed foods, and in with the new wave of naturally hued, whole foods as a holistic approach to good health. She also recommended that I read the book, *The Hip Chick's Guide to Macrobiotics*. She joked that if the trend was working the rich and famous, it was worth a shot for us common folk. Humor aside, without a personal chef, a strict macrobiotics diet can be difficult to adhere to, though its principles have changed my life forever. After my first few days of brown rice, I gradually introduced simple foods like chicken Caesar salads, sans croutons or cheese. The results in the first few weeks were miraculous. My body began to function and my mind seemed crystal clear. I also had an abundance of energy. It was difficult to pinpoint exact foods that were deleterious; although it was apparent that I had a severe fiber deficiency, rather than celiac disease. It was also clear that I could not tolerate processed foods well; as whole oat groats became friend, while instant oatmeal was foe.

After 12 years as a Ph.D. chemist, my most surprising discovery to date remains that prayer and nutrition are capable of healing, if you are willing to work at it. While most doctors reputably give patients appropriate nutritional prescriptions; it is the patient's responsibility to put it into action. My dietician helped me do that.

German doctor, Christoph von Hufeland, was the first to publish a macrobiotics book in 1796. This diet was later presented, in 1970, to the U.S. Congress by Michio Kushi, a student of George Ohsawa. It focuses on Ohsawa's "Twelve Laws of Change of the Infinite Universe", whereupon aligning with God - we may feel inner peace and happiness through prayer, meditation, fellowship, and service. George watched his two younger sisters, brother, and Mother die of tuberculosis (TB). At age 15, he too came down with TB. Determined and faithful, George sought holistic treatment under the guidance of Dr. Sagen Ishizuka. In 1911, George had fully recovered from TB of the lung and colon. Crediting his revival to a diet of brown rice, vegetables, sea salt, and moderate oils, he dedicated his life to continuing Dr. Ishizuka's findings on the power of unrefined whole grains, coupled with the right balance of potassium and sodium, and acids and alkalines.

Simply put, macrobiotics is about balance - nothing in excess. George's laws of change are expressed in two opposing forces: yin (expansive) and yang (contractive). ☯ Michio's diet recommends daily percentages of macrobiotics food groups. Since macrobiotics is also about freedom; nothing is forbidden and life is meant to be enjoyed. For an in depth study, refer to the macrobiotics books given in References (page 269).

Food = Energy

Macrobiotics focuses on deriving energy from living foods, which include: whole grains, dried beans, vegetables, fresh fruit, seeds, nuts, and fermented foods. It recommends a daily intake of: grains (50 – 60 %), vegetables (20 – 25 %), beans (10%), sea vegetables (5 – 10 %), soups (5 – 10 %), and naturally fermented foods (5 – 10%). Macrobiotics cautions against refined sugar, chemically treated and processed foods, nightshade vegetables, and most animal products, except fish; classifying: animal foods, fruits, desserts, nuts, and seeds as occasional foods. Nightshade vegetables are high in alkaloids, and include potatoes, tomatoes, peppers, and eggplant. They can deplete the bones of some calcium and thought to redistribute it within our soft tissue; thus potentially resulting in kidney stones and arthritis. Many nutritionists argue their health benefits; so follow your doctors' recommendations prior to any major change in diet.

"Macro" Means Great, and "Bios" Means Life
Here is to Living a Great Life

In this book, I merely introduce many of the foods in a typical macrobiotic diet; but with no percentage guidelines or restrictions against, vegetables, sugar, dairy, or lean meat. The focus of this book is on health, happiness, and faith, rather than limitations.

Live Grains for an Active yet Peaceful Brain

We have reviewed the origin and health benefits for each of the major whole grains (beginning on page 94); though we have not yet discussed how they give us so much energy and why they make us feel so incredibly at peace. Carbohydrates are the fuel that our bodies require for energy. Whole grains are complex carbohydrates, opposed to sugar and white flour, which are simple carbohydrates. Whole grains encourage slow chewing and a relaxed state of mind. Regardless of how fast you chew, they specifically support sustained mental energy through a slow, steady rise in blood sugar to the brain, which is in stark contrast to insulin. They are also considered a near complete food as they contain: antioxidants, amino acids, fiber, minerals, vitamins, and fat. Whole grains are an excellent source of thiamine, thought to reduce the risk of Alzheimer's disease. Finally, many whole grains are packed with protein, though some are lysine poor and considered incomplete proteins. The good news is that when consumed with beans, the body converts them into a complete protein. Additional grain constituents and benefits will be reviewed when we mill them (see page 151).

Beans & Grains – A Nutritional Match Made in Heaven

Legumes, or beans, are edible seeds that grow in a pod; and encompass lentils, beans, and dried peas. While beans lack the amino acid methionine, the body transforms them into high quality complete proteins when consumed with grains in the same day. Beans are packed with phytochemicals and protease inhibitors thought to prevent cancer. Besides whole grains, beans are one of the best sources of soluble fiber, which can alleviate constipation, lower cholesterol, and stabilize blood sugar. Beans provide an excellent source of iron, folate, manganese, copper, potassium, phosphorus, thiamine, zinc, magnesium, and vitamin B. Like whole grains, they are known to reduce the risk of heart disease, certain cancers, and arthritis. If beans induce gassiness, try soaking the beans overnight, discarding this water, and then cooking with a 2" strip of kombu (see sea vegetables on the following page).

Fermented Foods to Digest your Food

Fermented foods undergo the process of lacto-fermentation, whereby beneficial bacteria breaks sugars down to yield lactic acid, the natural preservative that lends a sour taste and tang. Examples include: miso, shoyu (soy sauce), sauerkraut, daikon or dill pickles, tempeh, natto, brown rice vinegar, umeboshi plums and their vinegar (Ume Plum), natural live yogurt, and pickled vegetables. Standard pickles are preserved in vinegar, chemicals, and additives; and are subjected to pasteurization rather than undergoing natural fermentation. Fermented foods strengthen your immune system and enhance overall digestive health. They contain enzymes and beneficial bacteria that inhibit the growth of harmful microbes and promote healthy flora in the intestines. In contrast, synthetic antibiotics kill off both good and bad intestinal bacteria. Greek yogurt, miso, and Ume Plum vinegar are my favorites, and are featured in this book.

Sea Vegetables as Super Foods & Kombu as Salt for your Grains

Seaweed are vegetables that grow in the sea. Sea vegetables include: Agar Agar, Arame, Dulse, Kombu, Nori, and Wakame, and can be found at your local health food stores. Seaweed offers a concentrated source of phytonutrients, chlorophyll, fiber, iron, zinc, vitamins (A, C, and the Bs), magnesium, and trace ocean minerals. They also contain spirulina and chlorella, which bind strongly with heavy metals and radioactive toxins; and thus, safely remove them from the body. Since seaweed also contains a balanced combination of sodium, potassium, calcium, phosphorus, and iodine, they may be used in place of salt (which can toughen grains or beans if added early in the cooking process). Many recipes herein begin with an optional 2" strip of kombu, rather than salt, for added flavor and nutrients. Add the kombu with uncooked grains or beans and water; cook, then discard. Wakame and nori are also favored and highlighted herein.

A Variety of Seaweed and Kombu (at right) after Infusion into Brown Rice

WHEAT BERRIES

The First Grain Salad I Experimented with & Still One of Our Favorites

Wheat Berry and Balsamic Broccoli Red Pepper Salad

For the Wheat Berries
- 2 cups wheat berries
- 3 ½ cups water
- 2 Tbs olive oil
- 2" strip kombu, *optional*

For the Salad (see Pantry for oils and vinegars, page 262)
- 1 head of broccoli, 2" pieces
- 1 Tbs sea salt
- 3 garlic cloves, minced
- ¼ + ¼ cup good balsamic vinegar
- ⅓ cup good olive oil
- 1 red pepper, ½" dice
- juice of ½ lemon
- 20 grinds of black pepper

Details: refer to Whole Grains Cooking Time Table (page 106) for optional methods
- Pressure cook the wheat berries in water and oil for 35 min on high; rapid release when the buzzer sounds (open the vent to depressurize); drain the water
- Add the broccoli to a mixing bowl; top with salt, garlic, and cooked wheat berries
- Add ¼ cup of balsamic vinegar and the olive oil to the wheat berries to infuse with flavor; cover to slightly steam the garlic and broccoli; cool to room temp
- Add the diced red peppers to the cooled wheat berry salad; the peppers will retain their gorgeous red color and crunch if you can wait for the salad to cool
- Finish by tossing the salad with the remaining ¼ cup of balsamic vinegar, lemon juice, and fresh ground pepper; serve at room temperature

NOTE on Wheat Berry Salad, Olive Oil, and Vinegar:
In the next few chapters, many of the cooked grains, legumes, and vegetables will be used in salads where the oils and vinegars are not heated. Refer to Stocking the Pantry (page 262), as your choice of ingredients will dictate the salad's final flavor. In this chapter, do not overcook the grains. Here, the wheat berries should be plumped enough to offer a satisfying bite. They should be cracked open just enough to soak up some of the dressing, yet sufficiently firm to yield a salad with a pleasing chew, rather than a soggy texture. This was the first grain salad I experimented with. It fueled a healthy obsession.

SPELT

Lemony Artichokes, Velvety Feta, Crunchy Pepper & Grain Goodness

Spelt Berries with Artichokes, Green Pepper, and Lemon Feta Salad

For the Spelt Berries
- 1 ½ cups spelt berries
- 2 ¾ cups water
- 2 Tbs olive oil
- 2" strip kombu, *optional*

For the Salad (see Pantry for oils and vinegars, page 262)
- 18 oz plain or marinated artichokes, halved
- 1 tsp sea salt
- 1 garlic clove, minced
- 3 Tbs good olive oil
- juice of 1 lemon
- 3 Tbs of champagne vinegar
- 1 green pepper, ½" dice
- 8 oz feta cheese, ½" cubes
- 20 grinds of black pepper

Details: refer to Whole Grains Cooking Time Table (page 106) for optional methods
- Pressure cook the spelt berries in water and oil for 15 min on high; rapid release when the buzzer sounds (open the vent to depressurize); drain the water
- Cool the spelt slightly, while preparing the vegetables, by spreading it out on a rimmed cookie sheet (a.k.a., quarter or half sheet pan), or in a large bowl
- Drain the plain or marinated artichokes; halve, and remove any tough edges
- Add the spelt, artichokes, salt, garlic, olive oil, lemon, vinegar, and green pepper to a large mixing bowl; toss gently so that the artichoke leaves remain intact
- Cool to room temperature so that the feta cheese will retain its shape; now add the feta cheese, mix gently, and serve at room temperature

NOTE on Spelt Salad:

This salad is the epitome of a Green Greek Grain salad. Spelt offers a sweeter wheat taste relative to wheat berries; thus combines perfectly with the tart lemon and feta. The varied textures of creamy artichokes, velvety feta, crunchy green peppers, and wholesome spelt make every garlicky, lemony mouthful one to savor. I find it great for dieting and daydreaming, as it coaxes me into chewing each bite very slowly. It is also delicious and filling; so a little goes a long way. Green peppers offer high levels of vitamin C. Artichokes are high in fiber, potassium, magnesium, and antioxidants.

KAMUT

Plump Kamut Pairs Perfectly with Stout Cherry Tomatoes & Fresh Parsley

Golden Kamut bathed in a Sunshine Hued Lemony Vinaigrette

Kamut with Lemon, Parsley, and Cherry Tomatoes

For the Kamut Berries

- 1 ½ cup Kamut
- 2 ¾ cups water
- 2 Tbs of olive oil
- 2" strip kombu, *optional*

For the Salad (see Pantry for oils and vinegars, page 262)

- 2 garlic cloves, minced
- 2 tsp sea salt
- 3 Tbs of white wine vinegar, such as Pinot Grigio based
- juice of 1 lemon
- 3 Tbs good olive oil
- 1 pint of cherry tomatoes, cut in half or thirds if large
- 1 head of Italian parsley, leaves only, chiffonade and minced, ~ 1 scant cup total

Details: refer to Whole Grains Cooking Time Table (page 106) for optional methods

- Pressure cook the Kamut in water and oil for 40 min on high; rapid release (open the vent to depressurize); draining should not be necessary; cool on a sheet pan
- Remove the stems from the parsley; chiffonade the leaves by grabbing the entire bunch and rolling or pinching into a ball; slice the ball into thin strips; now mince
- Add the cooked Kamut, garlic, salt, vinegar, lemon juice, olive oil, tomatoes, and parsley to a large mixing bowl; toss, and serve at room temperature
- Microwave leftovers for ~ 30 sec. to remove the chill from the tomatoes

NOTE on Kamut:

Kamut is the largest grain in the wheat family. When cooked, each gorgeous, golden, slender grain bursts with flavor upon every bite. Kamut's size and texture lends itself nicely to juicy round tomatoes; and its sweet flavor pairs perfectly with fresh, green, lemony parsley. This is one of the easiest grain salads to make; and it is super healthy. Tomatoes are high in lycopenes, vitamins C and A; and parsley is a good source of folic acid. Any good white wine vinegar works well here; although the Pinot Grigio grape based vinegars offer an additional level of flavorful complexity beyond just acidity.

BULGUR

Tarragon Leek Tabbouleh

For the Bulgur
- 2 cups coarse bulgur
- 3 ½ cups water

For the Tabbouleh (see Pantry for oils and vinegars, page 262)
- 1 Tbs sea salt
- 1 leek, minced
- 3 garlic cloves, minced
- ¼ cup white wine vinegar
- zest of 1 lemon
- juice of 1 + 2 lemons
- ⅓ cup of good olive oil
- 2 Tbs tarragon, minced
- 1 bunch curly-leaf parsley, chiffonade leaves and mince
- 1 green pepper, ½" dice
- 1 pint cherry tomatoes, cut in half or thirds if large
- 20 grinds of black pepper

Details: refer to Whole Grains Cooking Time Table (page 106) for optional methods
- Bring the bulgur and water to a boil in a saucepan; reduce heat to low; simmer for ~ 10 min; cover and remove from heat; let sit ~ 10 min; drain the bulgur if needed
    - Alternate method: bring 3 cups of water to a boil; add to 2 cups of bulgur in a heat proof bowl; cover to steam for ~ 45 min; drain if needed
- Add the salt, leeks, garlic, vinegar, lemon zest, juice of 1 lemon, and olive oil to the warm bulgur in a large mixing bowl; toss, cover, and cool in the refrigerator
- Remove the stems from the parsley; chiffonade the leaves by grabbing the entire bunch and rolling or pinching into a ball; slice the ball into thin strips; now mince
- Add the tarragon, parsley, green pepper, tomatoes, the juice of 2 remaining lemons, and black pepper to the salad; toss and serve at room temperature

NOTE on Bulgur and Tabbouleh:
Parboiling, drying, and cracking red or white wheat berries makes bulgur a quick cooking grain. The size of the cracked pieces will dictate the required cooking time. Tabbouleh (pronounced, tuh-boo-lee or tab-ooh-lay) is a deliciously nourishing grain salad, which is typically made with parsley, mint, and green onions. For something delightfully different, I substitute the mint and onion with lemony tarragon and mild leeks. Tarragon vinegar can be used as the white wine vinegar if you can't find fresh tarragon. For a main course, add a cup of chickpeas, or your favorite cooked bean.

FARRO

Hearty Farro with Flavorful Kalamatas & Fennel Infused Goat Cheese

Auburn Kalamatas add Hearty Flavor and Color

Farro with Kalamata Olives, Roasted Red Peppers, and Goat Cheese

For the Farro

- 1 cup farro
- 2 cups water

For the Salad (see Pantry for oils, vinegars, and olives, page 262)

- 1 tsp sea salt
- 1 garlic clove, minced
- 2 Tbs olive oil
- 5 Tbs good balsamic vinegar
- juice of ½ lemon
- ½ cup pitted Kalamata olives
- 2 roasted red peppers, ½" dice, ~ ⅓ cup total
- 2 Tbs pine nuts
- 4 oz herbed goat cheese

Details: refer to Whole Grains Cooking Time Table (page 106) for optional methods

- Bring the water and farro to a boil in a saucepan; reduce heat to med-low; cook uncovered at a steady simmer (constant low bubbling) for ~ 25 min
- Drain the farro and transfer to a large mixing bowl; add the salt, garlic, olive oil, and balsamic vinegar; cover and chill in the refrigerator
- Add the lemon juice, olives, and pine nuts to the chilled salad
- Gently crumble and fold in the goat cheese and serve

NOTE on Farro and Herbed Goat Cheese:

Italian farro, or emmer wheat, has a distinctly beautiful matte finish due to the pearling process it undergoes. The level of pearling dictates the color. White farro, or 'perlato', has little bran; whereas tan speckled, or 'semi-perlato' farro, retains more of its bran. Pearled farro offers a distinctly pleasing chew, does not harden when refrigerated, and cooks quickly relative to wheat, spelt, Kamut, and triticale, each of which has all of their bran intact. Hearty farro, pleasingly chewy in texture, pairs nicely here with intensely flavored, meaty Kalamata olives. Sweet and smooth little pine nuts, juicy red peppers and creamy goat cheese complete the salad. Purple Haze® goat cheese by Cypress Grove Chevre is an amazing herbed goat cheese topped with fennel pollen and lavender. This unique cheese was my introduction to fennel pollen (see Pantry, page 262) and the inspiration for Chris's Mandatory Potatoes (recipe on page 196).

RYE BERRIES

A Super Healthy, Strong & Bitter Sweet Salad, Akin to Korean Cuisine

Rye Berry Salad of Carrots, Radicchio, and Radishes

For the Rye Berries
- 1 ½ cups rye berries
- 2 ¾ cups water
- 2 Tbs olive oil
- 2" strip kombu, *optional*

For the Salad (see Pantry for oils and vinegars, page 262)
- 2 garlic cloves, minced
- 1 tsp red pepper flakes
- 2 tsp sea salt
- 10 grinds of black pepper
- 2 Tbs olive oil
- 4 Tbs sherry vinegar
- 2 carrots, very thin coins
- ½ head radicchio, chopped
- 6 radishes, very thin discs
- juice of 1 lemon

Details: refer to Whole Grains Cooking Time Table (page 106) for optional methods
- Pressure cook the rye berries in water and oil for 25 min on high; rapid release when the buzzer sounds (open the vent to depressurize); drain the water
- Add the cooked rye, minced garlic, red pepper flakes, salt, pepper, olive oil, and vinegar to the berries; toss, cover, refrigerate, and cool to room temp
- Add the carrots, radicchio, radishes, and lemon juice to the cooled, flavor infused, rye berries; toss and serve at room temperature

NOTE on Rye Berries:
Gorgeous sage green rye berries have a distinctly strong flavor, slightly sour and bitter, reminiscent of a good rye bread. Here, bold rye berries are paired with sweet carrots, bitter radicchio, and sharp, crunchy radishes. Finished with a spicy red pepper, citrusy, yet sophisticated sherry vinegar dressing; your palate will be wowed. Your body will also be rewarded thanks to rye's uniquely high levels of the fiber, arabinoxylan, known for its high antioxidant activity. Radicchio is high in vitamin K, radishes are rich in folic acid, and carrots are full of beta-"carot"enes (the orange provitamin our body converts to vitamin A). If you are new to grains and would like to blend rye with another grain, try a mixture of 50% wheat (pressure cook for 30 min on high) or 50 % spelt (pressure cook for 20 min on high). Allow for natural pressure release of either blend.

WHOLE HULLED BARLEY

The Grain that Saved my Body & Changed My Life

Barley with Greek Yogurt and Honey

For the Barley
- 1 cup whole hull-less barley
- 1 Tbs butter
- 1 ¾ cups water
- 2" strip kombu, *optional*

With Nuts and Seeds
- Greek yogurt
- pistachios
- roasted hazelnuts
- almonds
- sunflower seeds
- pumpkin seeds
- honey

With Fruit and Nuts
- Greek yogurt
- pecans
- brazil nuts
- dried dates
- dried cranberries
- dried coconut
- honey

Details: refer to Whole Grains Cooking Time Table (page 106) for optional methods
- Pressure cook the barley in water and butter (or olive oil) for 50 min on high; rapid release (open the vent to depressurize); draining should not be necessary
- Serve ~ ¼ of the cooked barley per person, or per day
- Top with Greek Yogurt (or milk) and your favorite fruits, nuts, and seeds
- Refrigerate leftovers in Tupperware, microwave grains alone for 35 sec to reheat

NOTE on Barley and Greek Yogurt:
This breakfast is what first and most decisively reversed my poor health (see page 17). Barley, my miracle grain, is substantial, chewy, pairs with almost anything, and offers more fiber (8 g / ¼ cup) (both soluble and insoluble) than any other gluten containing grains. Its mildly sweet flavor is a perfect match for tart Greek Yogurt topped with orange blossom honey and distinctively flavored richly textured pistachios. Greek Yogurt also aids in digestion, as it is an excellent source of enzymes and probiotics (beneficial bacteria). My favorite brand is FAGE (pronounced 'fa-yeh'). This authentic Greek Yogurt contains nothing beyond cow's milk, cream, and live active yogurt cultures. It is then strained to yield a thick, velvety texture unlike any other yogurt, which also results in a higher protein content.

OAT GROATS & FRIENDS BLENDS

Oat Meals for a Week that will Energize You - All Day, Every Day

Breakfast Blends for a Week

For the Oat Groats – Gluten-Free if pure and uncontaminated

- 1 ½ cups oat groats
- 1 ½ Tbs butter
- 2 ¾ cups water
- 2" strip kombu, *optional*

For the Oats Groats & Whole Grain Friends – Not Gluten-Free

- ½ cup whole oat groats
- ¼ cup rye berries
- ¼ cup spelt berries
- 1 Tbs millet grains
- 1 Tbs amaranth grains
- 1 Tbs of quinoa
- 1 Tbs teff grains
- 1 Tbs flax seeds
- 1 ½ Tbs olive oil
- 2 ½ cups water

Oat Groats Toppings

- macadamia nuts
- walnuts
- blueberries
- flax seeds
- sunflower seeds
- maple syrup
- brown sugar + milk or yogurt

Oat Groats & Friends Toppings

- cashews
- 2 dried figs, diced
- hemp seeds
- sesame seeds
- chia seeds
- pumpkin seeds
- honey + milk or yogurt

Details: refer to Whole Grains Cooking Time Table (page 106) for optional methods

- Pressure cook the Oat Groats in water and butter (or olive oil) for 35 min on high
- Pressure cook the Oat Groats & Friends in water and olive oil for 25 min on high
- Rapid release either by venting to depressurize; draining is not necessary
- Serve ~ ⅕ of the grains per person; plate with milk or yogurt and Toppings
- Refrigerate leftovers in Tupperware, microwave grains alone for 35 sec to reheat

NOTE on Cooking Time: Pressure cook the oats for 35 min for a hearty grain with a pleasing bite; or up to 45 min with an additional ¼ cup of water for a softer and chewier consistency. Or, stray from tradition and try the grain blend. The reduced cooking time does not overcook the smaller grains; and when added to milk, the result is a traditional cereal that allows you to taste and bite into each individual grain.

BROWN RICE

The Ultimate Comfort Foods – Brown Rice...

... and Brown Sugar & Rice Pudding

Perfect Brown Rice & Brown Sugar Rice Pudding

For the Brown Rice – GLUTEN FREE

- 1 cup short grain brown rice
- 2" strip kombu, *optional*
- 2 cups water

Details: refer to Whole Grains Cooking Time Table (page 106) for optional methods

- Add the rice and water to a saucepan; bring to a rolling boil; reduce the heat to low until simmering (a few bubbles per second); cover, and simmer for 40 min
- Fluff the rice; cover; let stand for 5 min; re-fluff and serve

For the Brown Sugar & Rice Pudding – GLUTEN FREE

- 1 cup short grain brown rice
- 2 cups water
- 2 ½ + ½ cup of favorite milk
- 2 Tbs butter
- dash of salt
- 1 tsp cinnamon
- 2 tsp vanilla
- ½ cup brown sugar

Details:

- Cook 1 cup of brown rice in 2 cups of water using the method above
- Add 2 ½ cups of milk, butter, salt, cinnamon, and vanilla to the cooked rice in its saucepan; heat on med and stir until the butter is melted; reduce the heat to low; cover and simmer for ~ 45 min until a thick porridge results
- Add the brown sugar; turn the heat off and stir in the remaining ½ cup of milk
- Allow the pudding to thicken by cooling a bit; serve at room temperature or hot

NOTES on Brown Rice:

There is a reason that so many baby foods are based on rice. It is gluten-free, soothing on the stomach, and easy to digest. When I eat brown rice, I tend to relax, chew slowly, and thank God for everything. Our friend, Lee Johnson, printed the beautiful note cards shown at left as a Thank You for his friends. Take the time to pen a note to your friends during your next bowl. *Thank you Lee!* Rice pudding is comfort food taken to the next level. This recipe was inspired by childhood weekends with my Grandma Hoyt.

SWEET BROWN SUSHI RICE

Ginger, Wasabi, Nori, Shoyu & Sweet, Sticky Brown Rice = Sushi for All

Ginger Perfumed Sweet Brown Sushi Rice

For the Sweet Brown Sushi Rice – GLUTEN-FREE
- 1 cup sweet brown rice
- 1 – 2" piece of fresh ginger
- 2 cups water
- ¼ tsp salt, or 2" strip kombu

Accouterments (see Pantry for sauces and nori, page 262)
- 2 Tbs rice wine vinegar
- 1 Tbs mirin (or sugar)
- wasabi roasted nori
- low sodium soy sauce

Details: refer to Whole Grains Cooking Time Table (page 106) for optional methods
- Slice the skin off of the ginger and whack it 'gingerly' with the flat side of a knife
- Add the rice, slightly smashed ginger, and water to a saucepan; stir, and bring to a rolling boil; reduce the heat to low until simmering; cover, and simmer for 40 min
- Fluff the rice; cover; let stand for 5 min; re-fluff and serve
- Add the rice to a mixing bowl; stir in the salt, rice wine vinegar, and mirin
- Serve wrapped within sheets of wasabi roasted nori, with soy sauce for dipping

NOTES on Sweet Brown Rice and Sushi:

Contrary to popular belief, the word 'sushi' does not mean raw fish. Rather, it means sour tasting, and refers to any dish prepared with "vinegared rice". This translation solidifies that fact that sushi is for anyone; as no raw meats, tempura-fried foods, or exotic toppings are necessary. Sweet brown rice differs slightly from medium or short grain brown rice in that it is rounder, shorter, and paler in color. When cooked, it is particularly sweet, plump, and sticky – perfect for rolling within nori. Here, I simply perfume the rice with ginger while cooking and infuse the cooked rice in a sweet mirin and tangy rice wine vinegar bath. With a dash of soy sauce (or shoyu), and pack of wasabi roasted nori, I have a satisfying and über healthy lunch. I have enjoyed writing this book as I love new discoveries, and wasabi roasted nori (seaweed, page 110) is no exception. I discovered this healthy treat on a business trip in San Diego with my fab foodie-friend Ann Goette, and we made it a mission to find these at home. Look for them in your grocery market or inquire at your local heath food store.

ROMANTIC RICE

Exotic Jasmine Perfumed Brown, Rustic Red & Forbidden Black Rice

Red, Forbidden, and Jasmine Rice

GLUTEN-FREE

For the Bhutanese Red Rice

- 1 cup red rice
- 1 ¾ cups water

Details: refer to Whole Grains Cooking Time Table (page 106) for optional methods
- Add the red rice and water to a saucepan; bring to a rolling boil; reduce the heat to low until simmering; cover, and simmer **for 20 min**
- Fluff the rice; cover; let stand for 10 min; re-fluff and serve

For the Black Forbidden Rice

- 1 cup forbidden black rice
- 1 ¾ cups water

Details: refer to Whole Grains Cooking Time Table (page 106) for optional methods
- Add the black forbidden rice and water to a saucepan; bring to a rolling boil; reduce the heat to low until simmering; cover, and simmer **for 30 min**
- Fluff the rice; cover; let stand for 10 min; re-fluff and serve

For the Brown Jasmine Rice

- 1 cup jasmine brown rice
- 1 ½ cups water

Details: refer to Whole Grains Cooking Time Table (page 106) for optional methods
- Add the brown jasmine rice and water to a saucepan; bring to a rolling boil; reduce the heat to low until simmering; cover, and simmer **for 40 min**
- Fluff the rice; cover; let stand for 10 min; re-fluff and serve

NOTES on Romantic Rice: If rice were the spice of life, we could enjoy a spicy life indeed. A myriad of unique varieties are available today with exotic colors (based on the bran color) and flavors. Bhutanese red rice is grown in the Himalayas at an altitude of 8,000 feet; and it is vigorously pearled. Its sweet flavor and thin bran layer make it a quick cooking and widely accepted rice by newcomers to whole grains. Legend has it that Black rice, or Emperor rice, was exclusively produced for royalty. It is also thought to offer health benefits for diabetes treatment in Chinese medicine. Brown Jasmine is a long-grain, slender, aromatic rice with most of its bran intact. Its delicate flavor and fluffy texture allows it to soak up sauces and pair with nearly any main course.

WILD RICE

What should you serve with Wild Rice? Wild Game...

Wild Rice   Brown Basmati Rice

Wild Rice and Brown Basmati Blend

For the Brown Basmati and Wild Rice Blend – GLUTEN-FREE

- ¾ cup of brown basmati rice
- ¼ cup of wild rice
- 2 cups water
- 2" strip kombu, *optional*

Details: refer to Whole Grains Cooking Time Table (page 106) for optional methods

- Add the wild rice, brown basmati rice, and water to a saucepan; bring to a rolling boil; reduce the heat to low until simmering; cover, and simmer for 45 min
- Fluff the rice; cover; let stand for 5 min; re-fluff
- Serve alone or with main course deglazed pan sauces

NOTES on Wild Rice and Brown Basmati:

Next time you cook with wild rice, study a few grains in the sunlight. It is simply stunning. Slender, long, and black as midnight - bronzed with glistening highlights of amber and auburn, who wouldn't want to eat this? Wild rice, as we know, is actually not rice, rather an aquatic grass (gluten-free grains, page 100). Its nutty and slightly earthy flavor and open texture when cooked make it the perfect vehicle for rustic, deglazed wine sauces. Good wild rice is typically hand harvested which makes it relatively expensive. I typically pair it with another grain to minimize expense. I find Brown Basmati rice to be the perfect complementary grain for wild rice. This long-grain, slender, rice cooks lends a wonderful aroma to the wild rice. Brown Basmati rice requires the same amount of cooking time as wild rice, as they contain their full bran layer.

Why add such a simple recipe to this book?

These two grains blend together impeccably, and they are the perfect sponge to soak up deglazed sauces (page 253). I love steak sauce, but you won't need it here. Shown at left is a thick cut of pan seared, oven roasted, salt and pepper crusted Venison Broil. The pan was deglazed with ⅓ cup of Cabernet Sauvignon. The venison took a total of 16 min to make: 1 min of searing on each side, 12 min in the oven, and 1 min to deglaze. I started the rice first. Next, I sliced the squash on the mandolin to prep the lemon pepper roasted squash. The squash recipe calls for an oven temperature of 400 °F; although you can certainly roast the venison alongside the squash – both at 380 °F or 400 °F. This is as simple as gourmet gets. It is healthier and tastes better than what you can get at most steak houses; though we may be biased.

QUINOA

Fun to Say & Better to Eat

Awesome Greenwa Quinoa

Greenwa Quinoa Cilantro Lime Serrano Salad

For the Quinoa – GLUTEN-FREE

- 1 ½ cups quinoa
- 2 ¾ cups water

For the Salad (see Pantry for oils and vinegars, page 262)

- 2 tsp sea salt
- 3 green onions, minced
- 4 Serrano peppers, ¼" dice
- 1 green pepper, ½" dice
- juice of 3 large limes
- 2 Tbs olive oil
- ½ bunch of cilantro leaves, minced and whole for garnish
- 4 Tbs white wine vinegar
- 2 avocados, diced

Details: refer to Whole Grains Cooking Time Table (page 106) for optional methods

- Add the quinoa and water to a saucepan; bring to a rolling boil; reduce the heat to med; cover, and simmer for ~ 13 min
- Remove from the heat; fluff; cover, and let stand for ~ 5 min
- Spread the quinoa out on a cookie sheet to cool a bit in the fridge or freezer
- Add the cooled quinoa, salt, green onions, Serrano peppers, green peppers, lime juice, olive oil, minced cilantro, and vinegar to a large mixing bowl; toss to mix
- Add the diced avocados; toss gently to maintain their shape
- Garnish with cilantro leaves and serve at room temperature

NOTE on Quinoa:

Quinoa (pronounced, keen-wa), sounds like green-wa, is a protein powerhouse. Packed with green ingredients, this recipe is aptly named. Crispy green and spicy Serrano peppers are noticeably crunchy, juxtaposed against the dainty discs of quinoa, and semi-firm chunks of buttery avocado. Deseed the peppers to your spice tolerance (see Lessons, page 253). You can differentiate the separated tender germs (the comma shapes) from their semi-crunchy seeds (period shapes) in each mouthful. This separation indicates that the quinoa is fully cooked. The dressing of fragrant green onions, lime juice, tangy vinegar, and cilantro is delicious.

MILLET

Sweet Delicious Dill Salad

Definitely Not for the Birds

Millet Pilaf with Heirloom Tomatoes and Dilled Sweet Corn

For the Millet – GLUTEN-FREE
- 1 cup millet
- 1 Tbs olive oil
- 2 cups water

For the Salad (see Pantry for oils and vinegars, page 262)
- 2 ears of sweet corn kernels
- 2 medium tomatoes, 1" dice
- 2 tsp sea salt
- 2 garlic cloves, minced
- juice of 1 lemon
- 2 Tbs olive oil
- 4 Tbs apple cider vinegar
- 1 Tbs fresh dill, minced

Details: refer to Whole Grains Cooking Time Table (page 106) for optional methods
- Toast the millet by adding it to a dry sauté pan set on med heat
- Shake the pan continuously for ~ 4 - 5 min, to prevent burning, until the millet is lightly golden, fragrant, and begins to pop
- Bring the water to a rolling boil in a saucepan; add the olive oil and toasted millet; reduce the heat to low; cover, and simmer for ~15 min until the water is absorbed
- Turn off the heat; fluff the millet; cover, and let stand for 5 min
- Transfer the cooked millet to a rimmed sheet pan to cool to room temp
- Place the corn cobs in a saucepan; add water to 2" over the corn; bring to a boil; reduce heat to med; boil gently for 3 min; transfer the cobs to a large bowl with ice water; cool for ~ 5 min to preserve their color; drain, and slice the kernels off
- Marinate the diced tomatoes with the salt, garlic, lemon, olive oil, vinegar, and dill in a large mixing bowl; add the millet and corn; toss and serve at room temp

NOTE on Millet:

Millet is commonly known for its inclusion in birdseed blends. Though, it ought be universally known as the highest fiber containing, gluten-free, grain at 9 g / ¼ cup. It is sweet and enchanting with its ever so slightly crunchy texture. Its appetizing bite pairs particularly well here with sweet crunchy corn enrobed in cider vinegar marinated sweet tomatoes and piquant dill. Or, try substituting ~ 3 Tbs of minced basil for the dill.

BUCKWHEAT

Bold Buckwheat & Glistening Garlic in an Asian Fusion Salad

Buckwheat with Cremini Mushrooms, Roasted Garlic & Micro Greens

For the Buckwheat – GLUTEN-FREE
- 1 cup buckwheat groats, unroasted, pale in color
- 1 egg, whisked
- 1 ¾ cups water

For the Roasted Garlic
- 1 head of garlic with skin on
- 2 Tbs olive oil
- 1 tsp sea salt
- 3 grinds of black pepper

For the Mushroom Sauté
- 10 cremini mushrooms, sliced
- 2 Tbs olive oil, 1 Tbs butter
- 1 tsp sea salt
- 2 Tbs rice wine vinegar

For the Salad (see Pantry for oils and vinegars, page 262)
- 1 tsp sea salt
- 10 grinds of black pepper
- 2 Tbs rice wine vinegar
- 3 Tbs white wine vinegar
- juice of 1 lemon
- 2 cups micro greens
- 6 baby turnips, thin coins
- 1 tsp sesame seeds

Details:
- Roast the garlic and sauté the mushrooms (details on pages 141 and 142)
- Whisk an egg in a medium mixing bowl; stir the buckwheat groats to coat
- Heat a nonstick sauté pan over med heat; add the egg coated groats; stir for ~4 min until dry, while breaking up most of the clumps
- Bring the water to a boil in a saucepan; add the egg enshrouded groats, simmer for ~10 min; drain and transfer to a rimmed cookie sheet; cool to room temp
- Add the groats, roasted garlic (skin removed) and its oil, sautéed mushrooms and the remaining salad ingredients to a large mixing bowl; toss the salad gently to preserve the garlic cloves' shape; serve warm or at room temperature

NOTE on Buckwheat Groats: Buckwheat's earthly flavor and rich texture pairs beautifully with buttery roasted garlic. Crisp baby turnips and sautéed mushrooms provide a lovely contrast. Delicate micro greens and rice vinegar lighten and brighten the salad. Micro greens (tiny young vegetable leaves) can be substituted with sprouts.

Whole Roasted Garlic Cloves

For the Roasted Garlic

- 1 head of garlic with skin, top removed, or sliced in half
- 2 Tbs olive oil
- 1 tsp sea salt
- 3 grinds of black pepper

Details: Preheat oven to 375 °F (roast)

- Slice the top root off the garlic, or cut the bulb in half to expose all of the cloves
- Drizzle with olive oil, salt and pepper; bake in a tin-foil covered pan for 45 min
- Gently squeeze the cloves out of their skin, or use a fork to help coax them out

NOTE: Whole garlic cloves may be too large for some. Slicing softened, butter-like cloves after roasting can crush their shape and dull their color; whereas, halving the entire bulb prior to roasting results in a beautiful mixture of whole and halved cloves.

Sautéed and Deglazed Mushrooms

For the Mushroom Sauté

- 15 - 30 fresh mushrooms, sliced
- 2 + 1 Tbs olive oil
- 1 tsp sea salt
- 2 - 3 Tbs rice wine vinegar

Details:

- Heat 2 Tbs of olive oil in a sauté pan
  on high until shimmering; add the mushrooms, sauté for ~ 3 min until golden
- Add the salt, reduce the heat to med or med-high depending on the quantity;
  add 1 Tbs of olive oil if needed; sauté for ~ 3 - 5 min until the natural juices release
- Add the vinegar and scrape the pan to deglaze the mushroom bits; this will plump
  the mushrooms roughly back to their original size, and infuse them with flavor

NOTE: Cremini, shitake, portabella, and white button mushrooms all work well here.
Use your favorite vinegar or wine as the deglazing liquid (see page 253).

AMARANTH

The Caviar of Whole Grains

Amaranth Polenta with Sugar Peas, Shitakes, and Sun-Dried Tomatoes

Dedication: To Dr. Susan Willis, my caviar of friends. Amaranth, the caviar of grains, and Susan, each have so much more to offer than good looks and taste. Susan and I share a Christian bond, love of food, shopping, and all things positive. She also gave me the encouragement I needed to stick to the original concept of a spiritual cookbook.

For the Amaranth Grains – GLUTEN-FREE

- 1 cup amaranth
- 1 ½ cups water (after sauté)

For the Polenta (see Pantry for oils and vinegars, page 262)

- 2 + 1 Tbs olive oil
- 20 shitake mushrooms, sliced
- 2 tsp sea salt
- 2 garlic cloves, thinly sliced
- juice of ½ lemon
- ⅓ cup Pinot Grigio white wine
- 1 cup fresh sugar snap peas, with or without shells
- ¼ cup sun-dried tomatoes, ½" dice, oil drained
- ¼ cup Parmigiano Reggiano
- 10 grinds of black pepper

Details:

- Heat 2 Tbs of olive oil in a sauté pan on high until shimmering; add the sliced mushrooms, sauté for ~ 3 min, add 1 more Tbs of olive oil to prevent scorching
- Reduce the heat to med; add the salt and garlic slivers; sauté for another ~ 4 min
- Add the lemon juice and white wine (or 1 Tbs white wine vinegar); scrape the pan to deglaze the mushroom bits; add the water; increase heat to high; bring to a boil
- Add the amaranth; stir gently; reduce heat to low; cover and simmer for ~ 15 min
- Add the fresh peas, sun-dried tomatoes, Parmigiano, and pepper
- Cook until desired thickness, ~ 4 min longer for soft polenta, and serve

NOTE on Amaranth:

This polenta exudes luxury, with its distinct silken texture, due to Amaranth's viscous starch (amylopectin). Each silky amaranth grain explodes with flavor and offers the slightest crunch alongside peas that burst with sweetness. The sun-dried tomatoes and mushrooms enrich the meal, all enveloped in a creamy, citrusy, salty Parmigiano base.

TEFF

Beefsteak Vinegar & Tomatoes Break Caprese Balsamic Tradition

The Teff Tart Serves as a Hearty & Beautiful Serving Vehicle

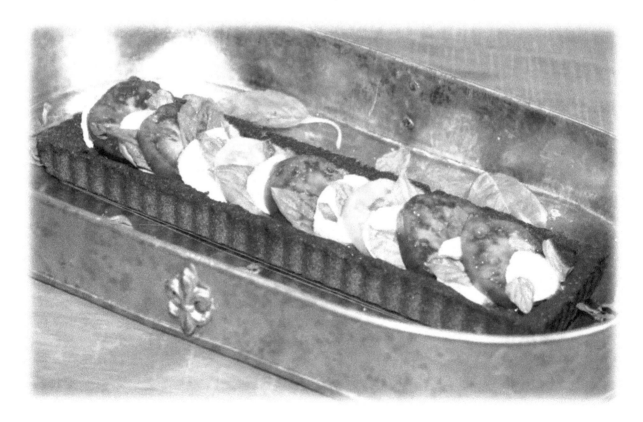

Teff Caprese Tart with Beefsteak Vinegar and Tomatoes

For the Teff Tart – GLUTEN-FREE
- 1 cup teff grains
- 3 cups water
- 1 Tbs butter
- 1 tsp sea salt

For the Caprese Salad Tart Assembly (see Pantry for vinegar, page 262)
- 1 lb of fresh mozzarella, buffalo is best, ¼" slice
- ~30 fresh basil leaves
- 3 beefsteak tomatoes, ¼" slice
- 2 Tbs fresh oregano leaves
- 4 Tbs good olive oil
- 4 Tbs Ume Plum Vinegar
- 30 grinds of black pepper

Details: Preheat oven to 350 °F after the molded teff tart has chilled
- Bring the water to a boil; whisk in the teff to break up initial clumps; reduce the heat to low; cover, and simmer ~ 25 min; stir a few times to prevent clumping
- Whisk in the butter and salt; cook to thicken to a spreadable consistency, ~ 3 min; spoon the teff into a greased 4" x 14" tart mold; press the polenta with a spatula to form walls to the top of the mold, and a base ½ of the thickness of the walls
- Cover the filled mold with saran wrap; chill for ~1 hr in the refrigerator to firm
- Bake the tart for 30 min; cool ~ 10 min on a wire rack; remove tart from the mold
- Fill the cooled teff tart with the Caprese salad by alternating slices of mozzarella cheese, basil leaves, and heirloom tomato slices, as shown at left
- Finish the salad by topping with oregano and drizzle with olive oil, ume plum vinegar (or, if preferred, balsamic vinegar with a dash of salt), and pepper

NOTE on Teff: Teff is the tiny grain from Ethiopia. As flour, it is used to produce Ethiopian flat bread (injera) with a porous texture perfect for dipping in sauces. Here, the grains are formed into a firm polenta as the carrier for a tangy Caprese salad with a twist. Ume Plum vinegar (try Eden Foods') is the pickling brine of umeboshi plums and red shisho (aka, beefsteak leaf); hence the humor in pairing it with beefsteak, heirloom tomatoes. The mozzarella, tomato, and vinegar quality are all-important here. Try this tart with a variety of fillings; chilled, or grilled to melt your beloved cheese.

CORN GRITS

A Celebration of Color, Texture, Flavor & Milestones

Jalapeño Smoked Cheddar Blue & Yellow Corn Grits

For the Blue or Yellow Corn Grits ~ GLUTEN-FREE

- 1 cup coarse grind cornmeal
- 2 cups chicken broth
- 2 cups milk, whole or 2%
- ½ tsp salt

For the Jalapeño Sauté and Cheese Infusion

- 3 Tbs butter
- 3 jalapeños, ¼" dice
- 1 tsp sea salt
- 4 oz smoked cheese, grated
- 6 baby chives, minced
- drizzle of pure maple syrup

Details:

- Heat the chicken broth and milk in a saucepan on high; bring to a boil; whisk the cornmeal while pouring it in to the boiling liquid to prevent clumping; add the salt
- Reduce the heat to low; cover, and simmer for ~ 40 min
- Add the butter to a sauté pan; heat on high until melted and just bubbling; add the jalapeños and salt; reduce the heat to med; sauté for ~ 6 min until tender
- Gently stir the sautéed jalapeños and its butter into the cooked grits
- Add the grated cheese to the grits and gently whisk to break up any lumps
- Serve hot and garnished with baby chives and a drizzle of maple syrup

NOTE on Corn Grits, Cornmeal, and Polenta:

Raised in NE PA, yet having spent the second half of my life in SW VA; I have not made grits until recently. Though more common to the Deep South, every household should have a great grits recipe. On a business dinner in Fort Worth, TX with NanoSonic's CEO, Dr. Richard Claus, we celebrated my 10 year anniversary with NanoSonic at Reata Restaurant. Famous for their jalapeño cheddar grits, they provide an equally warm, yet rustic ambience. No inch of the walls is spared from Texan taxidermy horns or hunting relics, ranging from present day artillery to medieval chain mail armor. In appreciation of this milestone memory and Rick's invaluable mentorship, I made it a mission to recreate these grits. This is my healthy reincarnation. Feel free to replace the milk with heavy cream. Any cheddar or smoked cheese works here, though Beecher's Smoked Flagship from Seattle is my favorite. Luckily, our local grocery and health food stores carry it.

Give us this day our daily bread.

And forgive us our debts, as we forgive our debtors. And lead us not into temptation, but deliver us from evil: For thine is the kingdom, and the power, and the glory, for ever Amen. For if ye forgive men their trespasses, your heavenly Father will also forgive you: But if ye forgive not men their trespasses, neither will your Father forgive your trespasses.

~ Matthew 6:11-15 KJV

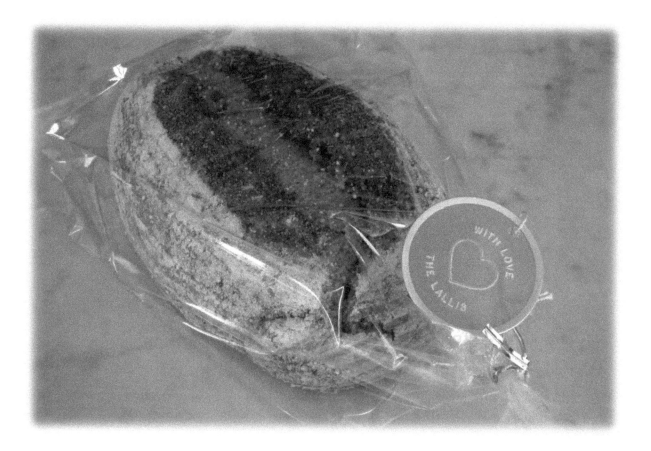

And Jesus said unto them, I am the bread of life: he that cometh to me shall never hunger; and he that believeth on me shall never thirst.

~ John 6:35 KJV

Chapter 3: For the BREADLERS

- WHOLE GRAIN BREAD BASICS

- o Milling: the Whole Grain into its Healthy Components
- o Why Mill Your Own Grains?
- o Whole Grains Bread Laboratory
- o Step-by-Step Breadling

- o **100% WHOLE WHEAT BREADS**
  - Multigrain Brick Oven Boule
  - Millet and Chia Seed Sandwich Rolls
  - Whole Grain Venison Heroes
  - Fig, Flax, and Hemp Seed Breakfast Bread

- o **WHOLE GRAIN CRACKERS**
  - Wheat Hearts
  - Fleur de Rys

- o **WHOLE WHEAT PASTA**
  - Whole Wheat Pasta Dough

- o **WHOLE WHEAT TORTILLAS**
  - Whole Wheat Soft Taco Shells

- o **A WHOLE LOT OF FUN**
  - Triticale Caraway Soft Pretzels
  - Whole Wheat Popovers with Blackberry Honey Butter

- o **ULTIMATE WHOLE WHEAT TREATS**
  - Gluten-Free Chocolate Poeuffs & Maple Almond Poeuffs
  - Blackberry Mojito Quick Bread
  - Mini Carrot Cupcakes & Cream Cheese Icing

Milling: Delving Deeper into the Whole Grain

Milling the Whole Grain into its Healthy Components

Endosperm - makes up ~ 83% of the kernel. Comprised of starch, protein, and Moisture; it feeds the germ's embryo, once sprouted.

Germ - makes up ~ 3% of the kernel. It contains the embryo, soluble and insoluble fiber, essential vitamins, minerals, and oils.

Bran - or pericarp, makes up ~ 14% of the protective portion of the kernel. It is comprised of layers of carbohydrate/cellulose insoluble fiber, vitamins, and minerals. The most nutritious and largest layer, the aleurone, is high in niacin, and lies next to the endosperm.

A whole grain is defined as a kernel that has 100 % of its three edible components intact: bran, endosperm, and germ. According to the Whole Grains Council, a food may be only labeled as a whole grain product if the processed grain (milled, cracked, rolled, cooked, etc.) delivers approximately the same balance of nutrients as the original seed.

1. the Endosperm – to Prevent Type-2 Diabetes

The endosperm is the largest portion of the grain and consists of about 75% starch (amylose and amylopectin), protein, and B vitamins, which serve as nourishment for the germ. Its unrefined, high quality carbohydrates slow the absorption of sugar into the bloodstream, and thereby counter insulin resistance. Replacing refined sugars and processed foods with unrefined carbohydrates is known to prevent type 2 diabetes.

2. the Germ – for Cardiovascular Health

The germ, or the heart of the kernel, contains heart-disease preventing B vitamins, such as B9 (folic acid), B1 (thiamin), and B6 (pyridoxal phosphate). It also contains omega-3 fatty acids, vitamin E (a powerful antioxidant which slows the oils from spoiling), fiber, essential minerals, and phytochemicals. This vital component contains the embryo, which when sprouted, forms new life; first as blades of grass, then as a new seed crop.

3. the Bran – for Digestive Health

The bran is a concentrated source of fiber that lowers cholesterol and purifies the digestive tract. It protects the kernel from insects and bacteria, and is high in B vitamins.

Why Mill Your Own Grains?

Health - As we now know, commercial wheat flours are produced by milling red, white, soft, or hard whole wheat kernels. The name and color (whole wheat, all-purpose white, self-rising, bread, cake, etc.) depend on the type of grain milled, the amount of bran and germ removed, and any potential additives. Whole grains beyond wheat are milled to yield a variety of gluten containing (ideal for bread) or gluten-free flours. Since home-milled grains maintain 100 % of the endosperm, bran, and germ; they officially qualify as whole grain flours. Some grains also contain a fourth component, an inedible hull, which must be removed prior to milling or consumption. Recall from our review of barley that the hulling process can remove some of the bran, as it is very tightly bound. Pearling also removes some, or all, of the bran (refer to barley and farro, page 94).

Since the germ lies just under the bran, if the bran is removed, so is the germ – the two most nutritious components of the kernel. All-purpose white flour is ground from the endosperm alone. The germ is intentionally removed to prevent the flour from going rancid. This occurs when the germ's oil (healthy unsaturated fatty acids) oxidizes upon exposure to air. Oxidation commences as quickly as 3 days and is complete over 6 - 9 months. While degermination yields flours with much longer shelf lives, it removes some the grain's essential vitamins and minerals. To account for this, manufacturers "enrich" white flour by adding iron, niacin, thiamin, riboflavin, and folic acid to the milled product, which results in similar nutritional profiles for whole wheat and unbleached all-purpose flour. Major benefits of whole wheat flour are its significantly higher fiber content and increased levels of protein, potassium, calcium, magnesium, phosphorus, and selenium.

Taste – While home-milled grains undoubtedly yield the freshest flour, they also may produce the healthiest, best tasting bread and baked goods that you will ever enjoy. My friends and I agree that freshly milled flours lend a distinctly sweet and nutty flavor. If you aren't ready to mill your own grains, rest assured that commercial and locally milled flours are nutritionally viable and fresh, as long as the store has a high turnover.

Enzymes – The major difference in home-milled flour is that it retains more enzymes. These live proteins catalyze biochemical reactions important to digestion. While they are heat sensitive and do not remain active in foods cooked at high temperatures; enzymes play two critical roles in whole grain bread production: 1) they break down the dough's starch molecules, and 2) lend uniquely complex flavors to the finished loaf.

Cost - Whole grains are living foods. While sensitive to air, light, and heat; they can be stored for years in an oxygen free, cool, dark environment (recall Joseph, see page 91). I purchase grains in 25 lb bags (~ $12 - $25) and store them in 5 gallon buckets (< $8) with oxygen absorber packets (< $1) sealed shut with gamma lids (~ $8) in our basement. For daily use, I store 2 – 10 lb quantities of various grains in airtight Oxo Pop containers in kitchen drawers or behind pantry doors. After the one-time, long-term storage investment of ~ $17, I can bake > 25 loaves of artisan whole grain bread for < $1 per loaf. Additional ingredients for bread include: water (milk or yogurt), yeast, salt, sugar (honey, molasses, and or fruit), oil (olive, vegetable, or butter), and limitless healthy additions (nuts, seeds, olives, fresh vegetables, etc.), so the final budget is up to you. Milling at home also eliminates the guesswork on shelf life. I grind what is needed for the day and refrigerate leftover flour in an Oxo container at room temperature for several weeks, or in a Ziploc bag in the fridge for several months. I store whole grain flours purchased from local health stores the same way. Flour may also be frozen. Storage is completely up to you. If the flour smells sweet and nutty, use it. If it lacks a distinct aroma, it is safe to use. Like any other food, it if does not smell appealing, do not use it.

Simplicity - Milling is beyond easy and complete within 3 steps. 1) Add grains to the hopper, 2) turn the power on, and 3) adjust the fineness of the grind if needed as the flour is produced. Bake, store, or give extra flour to those in need.

FUN - Become a Breadler - A breadler is someone so passionate about bread making that they begin peddling it with the intent to inspire new breadlers. I became a breadler 3 years ago and fast friends with our neighbor, Annie Krull, while delivering bread to another. Annie, a cancer survivor, explained that her doctor also recommended a diet rich in whole grains and low in processed foods. With a  shared love of baking and health, we headed to a bread making class at The Grain Mill in Wake Forest, NC. We returned with 100 lbs of grain and a lifelong Christian bond. Annie and her husband Dick are an inspiration. They exemplify marriage, faith, and charity. We hunt, pray, and 'break bread' together on a regular basis. Annie, never a victim, rather a prayer warrior, is my angel who ultimately taught me to 'Let go, and let God'.

Whole Grains Bread Laboratory

Precision ~ One of the best reasons to mill grains at home is that it fosters creativity. With your favorite grains on hand, you can start your own whole grain mini-bakery and laboratory. First, you can mill as much or as little as you like; and blend a variety of flours without having to purchase 1 to 5 lb bags when you may only need a quarter cup. This solves the issues of storage and spoiling. Second, milling your own grains allows you to control the amount of bran within your baked goods. Finally, you can adjust the fineness of your grind with a home mill to produce breads and baked goods with a variety of textures. A prime example of bespoke bread is pain Poilâne®. This famous French Miche (a round country loaf) is a hefty 2 kg levain (sourdough) based on two types of stone ground grains (70% wheat and 30% spelt), and a precise extraction of bran from the wheat (Type 85). Roughly 15% by weight of the larger bran particles are sifted and removed, which results in a 'transitional', rather than 100% whole grain bread. Today, more than 10,000 loaves of pain Poilâne are produced daily. The recipe has not changed since 1932 when Pierre Poilâne opened his initially humble Parisian boulangerie.

Bran ~ To learn more about the fineness of your grind, try sifting equal amounts of several types of flour and weigh the bran that remains (the particles that do not pass through the sieve). First, compare store-bought (all-purpose white, whole wheat, and cake flour) verses home milled (hard red and soft white wheat). Next, try sifting with different mesh flour sieves (fine, medium, or coarse). All recipes in this book were developed for 100% whole grain flours (sifting is not required). If you choose to sift out some of the bran, reserve it as an addition to the whole grain breads or cereals herein.

Variety ~ Major wheat varieties (hard or soft, red or white, and winter or spring) differ primarily in protein content, as dictated by their sowing season and region. Recall that hard wheat offers higher protein levels, which is best for strong gluten, CO_2 capturing networks in breads and lofty popovers; whereas soft wheat is ideal for tender cakes and chewy cookies. White wheat differs from red in that it has less red pigment in its bran. Lighter in color and flavor, it is a good option for those new to whole grains. Average protein ranges for 7 major classes of wheat follow: hard red spring (12 - 15%), hard red winter (10 – 14%), soft red winter (8.5 – 10.5 %), durum (12 - 15 %), hard white spring (10 - 15 %), hard white winter (10 – 14%), and soft white winter (8.5 – 10.5 %). Try other grain species reviewed earlier with varied gluten and protein contents for diverse flavors and health benefits. Gluten-free sorghum flour is a favorite and featured herein.

Yeast – The bread recipes in this book use **"instant yeast"**, also called: "fast-rising" or "fast-acting". Popular brand names include: Fleischmann's RapidRise®, RedStar® Quick-Rise™, SAF® Gourmet Perfect Rise, SAF Instant Red, and SAF Instant Gold. Instant yeast differs from "active dry" yeast in that no proofing is required (in hot water and sugar), thus the granules may be added directly to a recipe's wet or dry ingredients.

Options – The ingredients in each bread recipe are flexible, and I encourage you to experiment. For the **whole grains**, choose small grains, such as millet, amaranth, quinoa, or teff. Large whole grains (wheat, barley, or oat groats) may be incorporated into the dough, but must be sprouted or cooked prior. For the remaining constituents, the amounts are typically interchangeable as the dough is easily adjusted with flour and liquids. For the **hydrating liquids**, choose one or a blend of: water, milk, buttermilk, yogurt, soy, almond, or coconut milk. **Sugars** may be: white or brown, honey, agave nectar, brown rice syrup, sorghum syrup, maple syrup, or molasses. **Fats** include: olive oil, vegetable oil, canola oil, coconut oil, or melted butter. Add **healthy additions** such as: flax seed, chia seed, hemp seed, sesame seed, poppy seed, pumpkin seeds, and sunflower seeds. Each of these may be incorporated in the soak or final dough.

Guidelines: see whole grain flours in Lessons, page 253

- The recipes herein work for any shaped loaf or ~ 8 sandwich rolls (page 159).
- A 5 qt stand mixer with a 325 W motor will perform well. For doubled recipes, you will need a 6 qt bowl and more powerful motor (≥ 575 W) to handle the kneading.
- A bake stone will result in lofty, crisp, free standing loaves to mimic those from a hearth or brick oven; though it must be preheated at least 45 min prior to baking.
- Many recipes recommend transferring dough to a bake stone by thrusting it off of a pizza peel dusted with semolina, flour, or cornmeal. If too little flour is used, the dough will stick and can deflate after vigorous shoves. While flour from a banneton mold does not burn on your bread, it will smoke on a hot bake stone, and can over-brown the bottom of your bread. Thus, transfer dough to a bake stone by turning it gently onto parchment paper on a cutting board; then slide the paper from the board to the stone. The paper also simplifies oven rotating.
- Place a metal pan with 1 cup of water on the top rack ~ 15 min prior to baking the bread to create a steam bath for lofty loaves, up to ⅓ greater in height. "Oven spring" is the final rise that occurs in the first few minutes in the oven. The vapor slows crust formation, and gives the dough more time to release CO_2 and expand.

Step-by-Step Breadling

5-Step Breadling – Each whole grain bread recipe herein follows the same process: 1. Soak, 2. Mix, 3. Knead – Rest - Knead, 4. Rise – Pan - Rise, and 5. Bake – Cool - Eat.

Tools – 100% whole grain breads can be made without the **'need'** for special tools beyond mixing bowls, a wooden spoon, baking sheets, and an oven. Although, one **'want'** item I highly recommend is a large, nonstick pastry mat (starting at < $10). My favorite is the Silpat® Roul'Pat® (~$36). I use it daily to protect my countertops, and to knead or roll all types of dough. Since dough doesn't stick to the Silpat, it minimizes the temptation to over-flour. See **whole grain flours** in Lessons, page 253.

Method - Step 1, Soaking (8 hr), is the easiest, but takes the most time. Soaking all of the whole grains and some of the flour hydrates the bran and tenderizes the loaf. **Step 2, Mixing (~ 10 min)**, incorporates the soaked grains into the dough, and can be done by hand or with a stand mixer. While my stand mixer loaves are slightly loftier, doubling the kneading time for hand mixed dough ultimately produces similar results. **Steps 3 and 4, Kneading and Rising (~ 2 - 3 hr)**, are the "stress reliever" steps. Guidelines are given on timing; although I recommend that you relax and use common sense. Exercise, read, or run errands in between these steps; make adjustments to the dough rather than your day. **Step 5, Baking (~45 min)**, my favorite, involves adding toppings, transferring the panned or free form dough to the oven, cooling, and eating.

Step 1: Soak (~ 5 min to mix, and ~ 8 hr to soak)

- Mix all of the **Whole Grain Soak** ingredients together in a medium bowl with a wooden spoon; cover; let it sit for at least 8 hr, or up to ~ 24h, at room temp

Step 2: Mix (~ 10 min) by hand or with stand mixer

- Transfer the Soaked Whole Grains to a large mixing bowl or stand mixer
- Add the **Final Dough** Ingredients to the bowl with the Soaked Whole Grains
- **By Hand** - Mix with a wooden spoon or wet hands (minimizes sticking) for ~ 2 min until ingredients are assimilated, and a soft, slightly sticky dough results
- **With Mixer** - Stir with paddle attachment for ~ 1 min; scrape clean; replace paddle with dough hook; knead on low speed for ~ 3 min until a soft, slightly sticky dough forms; sprinkle in flour only if the dough sticks to the sides
- **For either method** – add flour or water to the bowl only if needed

Step 3: Knead – Rest – Knead (~ 10 – 15 min total)

- 3a – 1st Knead (4 min for stand mixer dough, or 8 min for hand mixed dough)
- Scrape the bowl; transfer all of the hand mixed or stand mixer dough to a floured countertop (or Silpat); sprinkle with flour; let it rest ~ 5 – 10 min; knead by hand:
  - **Flatten** - firmly push or gently pound with the palms of your hands
  - **Fold** - stretch and pull top end of the dough forward to meet the bottom
  - **Turn** – rotate the dough ¼ turn, or 90 ° counter-clockwise
  - **Repeat** – flatten, fold, turn (4 min for stand mixer, 8 min for hand mixed)
- Adjust the dough texture (to slightly tacky) during turns if needed
  - Sprinkle water, or dust flour, onto the dough only as needed; it should be supple, and slightly tacky, rather than overly sticky on your palms
- 3b: Rest – form a 'dough ball'; let it rest for ~ 5 min, uncovered at room temp
- 3c: 2nd Knead – knead dough for ~ 1 more min (~ 4 flattens, folds, and turns)
  - Make final adjustments with water or flour to pass the "windowpane" test
  - Stretch a small piece of dough thin enough for light to shine through it; if it tears easily, knead a few more minutes. Recall that bran tears gluten, and we are making 100 % whole grain bread; so do not obsess over this step
  - Form a dough ball for the next step when you are happy with the texture

Step 4: Rise – Pan – Rise (~ 2 hr total, depending on temp)

- 4a: 1st Rise in Bowl – transfer the dough ball to a lightly oiled bowl; cover; allow to rise at room temp until it is ~ 1 ½ times its original size (~ 45 – 60 min)
- while dough rises more quickly at elevated temperatures, do not exceed 90 °F
- 4b: Panning – transfer dough to a floured surface; shape (following 2 pages) per recipe: (round form for boule, loaf pan for sandwich, or free form for rolls)
- 4c: 2nd Rise in Pan – cover the dough loosely with saran wrap; preheat oven; allow the dough to rise at room temp to ~ 1 ½ times its size (~ 45 - 60 min)

Step 5: Bake – Cool – Eat (~ 45 min to transfer, top, and bake)

- Reduce - preheated oven temp (425 °F) to 350 °F (use a sticky note reminder)
- Transfer – free formed dough to a sheet pan or parchment paper for bake stone
- Add - steam bath ~15 min prior to baking, and toppings (egg and seeds) to dough
- Bake – per recipe; rotate half way through; remove when internal temp is 195 ° F
- Cool – transfer bread to a wire rack; cool at least 1 hr prior to slicing and eating
- Store – freeze, or store at room temp in a semi-open bag to prevent molding

Mixing, Kneading, Shaping, and Baking Bread

Soaking: Dried Figs, Flax, Whole Wheat Flour, and Small Grains

Mixing: Dough in 5 qt and 6 qt Stand Mixer Bowls

Resting: Dust Dough with Flour and Allow to Hydrate ~ 15 min

Kneading: 1) Flatten, 2) Fold, 3) Turn, and 4) Repeat

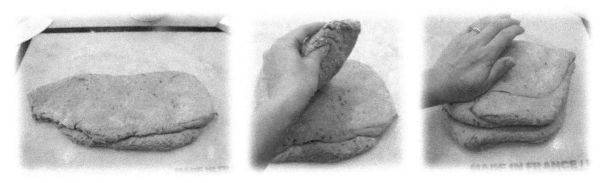

Then: Form a Dough Ball, Let it Rest, Knead Again, Try Windowpane Test

Forming a Dough Ball and a Free-Standing 'Boule':

In the 5-Step Breadling process a 'dough ball' is formed twice: first, during the 'rest' in between kneads, and second, during the first 'rise' in an oiled bowl. A dough ball is also formed during the final 'panning' process for a 'boule'. The Multigrain Boule herein is a round loaf, or miche (recall Poilâne, page 155), and formed using the following method:

- Flatten the dough into a square; fold the 4 edges (for a large boule) or the 4 small corners (for a small sandwich roll) or to the center; press to seal; pull the 4 remaining edges together; press to seam; roll to tighten the seam and form a ball
- Place the boule in a form (oiled bowl or floured banneton) **seam-side up** to rise

Forming Free Standing Sandwich Rolls, or a Baguette, or 'Batard':

The Millet and Chia Seed sandwich rolls are formed as either: 1) miniature flattened dough balls and sandwich loafs, or 2) as one large batard (French or torpedo roll):

- **Rolls:** divide risen dough into 6 – 8 sections and form mini boules or sandwich loafs; allow to rise on a nonstick bake sheet with the **seamed sides down**
- **Batard:** form risen dough into a rectangle; fold the longer edges to the center; bring the folded edges together; press to seal; roll to **taper the edges down**; transfer to a French bread pan, or parchment, with the **seam-side up** to rise

Forming a Sandwich Loaf for a 1 lb, 4 ½" x 8 ½" Bread Pan:

The Fig, Flax, and Hemp Seed breakfast bread in this book is formed into a sandwich loaf and baked in a standard bread pan using the following method:

- Flatten risen dough into a 5" x 7" rectangle with the 5" width facing you; roll the dough from the bottom to the top lengthwise; seal the edge by pinching the seam shut; roll the dough on the seam to smooth it; maintain an **even thickness**
- Transfer the dough to a loaf pan with the **seam-side down** to rise
- Allow the dough to rise ~ 1" above the top of the pan, cut a slash across the top to allow for expansion, and sprinkle on topping of choice (poppy seeds shown)

Score Dough with Serrated Knife, Brush with Egg Wash, Top with Seeds
Round Boule Baking on Parchment and Bake Stone under Steam Bath

Large, Rustic, Oval Batard Glistening on Cold Marble while Cooling

100% WHOLE WHEAT MULTIGRAIN BOULE

And he took the bread, and **gave thanks**, and brake it, and gave unto them, saying, This is my body which is given for you: this do in remembrance of me. Likewise also the cup after supper, saying, This cup is the new testament in my blood, which is shed for you.

~ Luke 22:19-20 KJV

Experiment: Make this bread with buttermilk first. This foolproof dough results in a deliciously dense bread perfect for dipping in hummus. Next, use water in the soak to learn how to change dough's texture with flour during the mixing and kneading steps. You will need ~ ½ to ¾ cup more to prevent sticking during the folds. If you can resist over-flouring, you will be rewarded with a lighter and stronger, moist sandwich bread.

Flax seeds: must typically be ground to obtain their full health benefits; though the soak here partially geminates them, allowing them to be used whole.

Multigrain Brick Oven Boule

For the Whole Grain Soak (the night before, or 8 hours prior)
Any combination of 16 Tbs of small grains or bran may be used

- 1 cup whole wheat flour
- 3 Tbs flax seeds
- 2 Tbs millet
- 2 Tbs amaranth
- 2 Tbs quinoa

- 2 Tbs oat or wheat bran
- 2 Tbs rolled oats
- 2 Tbs sesame seed
- 1 Tbs teff
- 1 cup buttermilk (or water)

For the Final Dough (the day of baking)

- 2 cups whole wheat flour
- 1 tsp salt
- 2 tsp yeast

- ¾ cup water
- 1 Tbs olive oil
- 2 Tbs honey

Topping: 1 egg beaten with 1 Tbs water, and poppy seeds

Details: Preheat oven to 425 °F (bake or bake stone) during rise; 350 °F while baking

- Follow Steps 1 – 4 of the 5-Step process (page 157) through the 1st ~ 45 min rise
- Form a 'boule' (page 159); transfer dough, seam-side up, to a well-floured banneton; cover; allow dough to rise to the top of the mold (~ 45 – 60 min)
- Gently turn the mold upside down to transfer the dough to a nonstick bake pan or a sheet of parchment paper (on a cutting board) if using a bake stone; cut ½" deep slits in the top of dough; brush with egg/water; sprinkle on poppy seeds
- Transfer bake pan to the oven, or slide the parchment paper onto a bake stone
- Bake at 350 °F for ~40 min with a steam bath (rotate after 20 min) until browned on all sides, or the internal temp is 195 °F in the center; cool on a wire rack for 1 hr

NOTE: Artisan Breadmakers produce gorgeous, rustic loaves of bread with striped patterns by allowing dough to rise in a well-floured banneton, also called a brotform. These wicker baskets (~ $30) are my second favorite bread tool. They are available as round (for a round boule), oval (for a wide batard), or long rectangular molds (for a narrow batard or French baguette, page 168). If you do not own a banneton, use a lightly oiled bowl. The loaf will not have floured stripes, although it will taste great. If using water in the grain soak, adjust the dough with flour (~ ½ - ¾ cup) more as needed.

SANDWICH ROLLS

When **Jesus** looked up and saw a large crowd coming toward him, he said to Philip, "Where can we buy enough bread for all these people to eat?" Another one of his followers, Andrew, Simon Peter's brother, said, "Here is a boy with **five loaves of barley bread and two little fish**, but that is not enough for so many people." Jesus said, "Tell the people to sit down." This was a very grassy place, and about **five thousand men** sat down there. Then **Jesus took the loaves of bread, thanked God for them**, and gave them to the people who were sitting there. He did the same with the fish, **giving as much as the people wanted**. When the **people saw this miracle** that Jesus did, they said, "He must truly be the Prophet who is coming into the world."

~ John 6:5,8-11,14 NCV

Millet and Chia Seed Sandwich Rolls

For the Whole Grain Soak (the night before, or 8 hours prior)
- 1 ⅓ cups whole wheat flour
- ¼ cup millet
- 3 Tbs chia or flax seeds
- 1 cup water

For the Final Dough (the day of baking)
- 2 ½ cups whole wheat flour
- 2 ½ tsp yeast
- 1 tsp sea salt
- ¾ cup water
- 2 Tbs honey
- 1 Tbs olive oil

Topping: 1 egg beaten with 1 Tbs water, and sesame seeds

Details: Preheat oven to 425 °F (bake or bake stone) during rise; 350 °F while baking
- Follow Steps 1 – 4 of the 5-Step process (page 157) through the 1st ~ 45 min rise
- Shape 6 – 8 sandwich rolls on a nonstick bake sheet, or 1 large batard (page 159); cover loosely; allow dough to rise on a bake sheet or in a mold for ~ 45 – 60 min
- Brush with egg, add sesame seeds; bake at 350 °F with a steam bath; small rolls for 25 – 28 min, or one large batard for ~ 40 min; rotate either half way through

HEROES

God Bless America,
Her unsung heroes, and amber waves of grain.

Whole Grain Venison Heroes

For the Venison Sauté
- ~ 1lb venison flank, 1" strips
- 2 Tbs olive oil
- 2 tsp sea salt
- 10 grinds of black pepper

For the Vegetable Sauté
- 2 Tbs olive oil
- ½ red onion, sliced thin
- 2 tsp sea salt
- 10 grinds of black pepper
- 3 mushrooms, sliced thin
- 1 red pepper, ½" wide strips
- 1 green pepper, ½" wide strips

For the Oven Baked Heroes
- 2 sandwich rolls, cut in half, center cut out if too thick
- ¼ cup banana peppers
- 2 slices provolone cheese

Details: Preheat oven to 400 °F (roast)
- Heat the olive oil on high in a sauté pan; add the flank steak strips, salt, and pepper to the pan and sauté until all sides of the meat is browned, ~ 6 min total; medium-rare will allow you to bite into the thickest of sandwiches
- Remove the venison from the heat. Either transfer the meat to a dish and add more olive oil to the sauté pan, or use a separate pan to sauté the vegetables
- Add the red onion, salt and pepper to the shimmering olive oil; sauté on high until tender ~ 4 min (caramelized, golden in color); add the mushrooms and peppers; sauté until the peppers are a bit charred, yet crisp ~ 3 min; remove from heat
- Cut two large pieces of sandwich rolls in half; remove some of the inside if the bread is too thick to bite into (our cat loves whole wheat bread, he gets this part)
- Arrange slices of flank steak on the bottom of each roll; top with sautéed vegetables, banana peppers, and provolone cheese, then the top half of the roll
- Roast at 400 °F to melt the cheese and crisp the bread, ~ 5 min

NOTE on Heroes: Heroes are tough, but your sandwich shouldn't be. Do not overcook the beef, and scoop out excess bread from the center if your rolls are extremely thick. Make this for your hero; and *tell them so.* Our nation will grow stronger as we continue to appreciate God, Country, and Family - in that order.

BREAKFAST BREAD

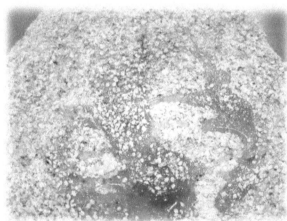

For the Fruit Soak (soak the night or 8 hr before, or simmer morning of)

- 4 dried figs, quartered
- 1 ½ Tbs flax seeds
- ¾ cup water (if soaking)
- *or* 1 cup water (if simmering)

Details:

- **Soak** the figs, flax seed, and water overnight; **OR** add to a saucepan; bring to a boil; reduce to low heat and **simmer** covered for 15 min; remove from heat

Fig, Flax, and Hemp Seed Breakfast Bread

For the Final Dough (the day of baking)
- the dried Fruit Soak (at left)
- ¾ cup Greek yogurt
- 1 ½ Tbs honey
- ¼ cup water
- 3 ¼ cups whole wheat flour

- 2 Tbs oat bran
- 1 tsp sea salt
- 2 ½ tsp instant yeast
- 6 Tbs hemp seed
- 3 Tbs sesame seeds

Topping: 1 egg beaten with 1 Tbs water, and poppy seeds

Details: Preheat oven to 425 °F (bake) during final rise, reduce to 350 °F while baking
- Puree the Fruit Soak in a food processor or blender until the figs are pulverized; whisk the puree together with yogurt, honey and water in a mixing bowl
- Whisk the flour, oat bran, salt, yeast, hemp seeds, and sesame seeds together in a separate mixing bowl to distribute the yeast; top with the fig mixture; follow Steps 2 – 4 of the 5-Step process (page 157) through the 1st ~ 45 min rise
- Form a 'sandwich loaf' (page 159); transfer dough, seam-side down, to a nonstick 1 lb loaf pan; cover; allow dough to rise ~ ½" above the pan (45 – 60 min)
- Cut a ½" deep slit along the top length of dough; brush with egg/water; sprinkle on poppy seeds; transfer the pan to the oven
- Bake at 350 °F for ~40 min with a steam bath (rotate after 20 min) until the top is browned, or the internal temp is 195 °F in the center; cool on a wire rack for 1 hr

NOTE: This recipe is for my breadler friends and dedicated to Annie. The name of this bread may sound funny, but it is delicious, super healthy, and makes the ultimate PB & J. The teeny tiny fig seeds lend the slightest crunch; while the yogurt imparts a distinctly moist texture that our friends' children love. Our adult friends adore the dense, yet tender and nutty flavored hemp seeds that round out the sweetness of the figs. Flax seeds were cultivated as far back as 3000 BC. They are high in dietary fiber (insoluble and soluble - including mucilage), lignans, and 'essential' omega-3 fatty acids, primarily, alpha-linolenic acid ('essential' since our bodies cannot synthesize them). Hemp seeds are packed with protein and contain all of the essential amino acids (as do chia seeds). Look for hemp seed in your local health food stores' refrigerated section. If needed, it can be substituted with ground pumpkin or sunflower seeds.

WHEAT HEART CRACKERS

We Whole-Heartedly Love these Whole Wheat Crackers

They even puff at the top corner, resembling a joy filled heart.

Wheat Heart Sesame Flax Crackers

For the Crackers (makes 4 dough discs for ~ 80 crackers, 2.5" tall hearts)
- 2 cups whole wheat flour
- ¼ cup pumpkin seeds, ground
- ¼ cup flax seeds, ground
- ¼ cup sesame seeds
- 2 tsp salt
- ⅔ cup water
- 2 Tbs honey
- 2 Tbs olive oil

Details: Preheat oven to 350 °F (convection bake) or (bake)
- Grind the pumpkin seeds and flax seeds separately in a food processor by pulsing until coarse flours result; do not over grind into a butter or paste
- Add the flour, ground pumpkin and flax seeds, whole sesame seeds, and salt to a large mixing bowl; whisk together to combine; add the water, honey and olive oil
- Mix with a wooden spoon until the flour just disappears; scrape all of the dough together and gently mold it into a disc; transfer to a nonstick surface (like Silpat)
- Slowly, but firmly, push and knead the dough ~ 2 min; it should not be sticky, or feel dry and crack when folded; extra flour and water should not be needed
- Form the dough into 4 discs; each may be rolled immediately, after a ~ 20 min rest covered at room temp, held overnight in the fridge; or, wrapped and frozen
- Roll each disc on a nonstick surface as thin as possible, ~ 1/16"; lift the dough and flip it over after every few rolls (at least 3 times before cutting) to help it stretch
- Cut out hearts with a cookie cutter; peel uncut dough away from hearts; transfer hearts to nonstick baking sheets using your hands or a thin metal spatula
- Bake 20 crackers per sheet, for ~ 12 min (convection bake), ~ 13 - 14 min (bake) until golden brown; cooking time increases with thickness; taste one to ensure that they are crisp, not burnt, or under-baked baked; cool on a wire cooling rack

NOTE: These crackers may be the most fun recipes in this book to make. The dough is silky smooth, easy to roll, re-roll, cut, and transfer. Think of this dough like your own clay to mold, soothingly yet firmly, just as God molds us. I make these for holiday and tea parties with cookie cutter shapes ranging from high heels to Halloween cats. They keep for 1 - 2 months in the fridge and are high in fiber and nutrients, making them a perfect snack for you or unexpected visitors. As a neutral base, they pair with nearly any cheese; or try the lemony Artichoke Pesto as a delicious healthy dip (page 222).

FLEUR DE RYS CRACKERS

Fleur De Rys Caraway Seed Crackers

For the Crackers (makes 2 dough discs for ~ 3 dozen, 3" tall fleurs)

- 1 ½ cup rye flour*
- 1 tsp salt
- 1 tsp baking powder
- 1 Tbs caraway seeds
- 3 Tbs butter, melted
- 1 Tbs honey
- ⅓ cup milk, cold (see note* before adding)

Details: Preheat oven to 350 °F (bake) or (convection bake) for a crisper cracker

- Whisk the rye flour, salt, baking powder, and caraway seeds in a mixing bowl
- Add the melted butter, honey, and milk; mix with a wooden spoon to form a ball; transfer the dough to a nonstick surface; knead it for ~ 1 min; form it into 2 discs
- The dough may be rolled immediately, after a ~ 20 min rest covered at room temp, or held overnight in the fridge; or, wrapped and frozen
- Roll each disc as thin as possible, ~ 1/16", on a nonstick surface lightly dusted with flour; roll from the center outward to prevent sticking to the rolling pin
- Cut the dough using a Fleur de Lys cookie cutter, or desired shape; peel the uncut dough away from the shapes; gently transfer the shapes to nonstick baking sheets (~ 18 per sheet) using your hands or a small, thin metal spatula
- Bake 18 crackers per sheet, for ~ 12 min until the edges are golden brown; cooking time increases with thickness; taste one to ensure that they are crisp, not burnt, or under-baked baked; cool the crackers on a wire cooling rack

NOTE: Cut as Fleur de Lys - these rye crackers had to be named - Fleur de Rys. Flecked with caraway seeds, and evocative of crisp buttery rye toast, they are perfect for dipping in hot Tafelspitz or Minestrone. They are also particularly delicious with soft blue Stilton, or goat cheeses; and pair well with stemmed caperberries, sun-dried tomatoes, and marinated artichokes. Recall that rye flour behaves differently from other flours (see gluten grains, page 94). * For very finely home milled rye, or Light Rye (i.e., Bob's Red Mill), follow the recipe above. For semi-coarse rye, with a slightly gritty texture, (i.e., Hodgson Mill® Rye), use ½ cup of milk (* rather than ⅓); allow the flour to hydrate in the bowl at least 10 min prior to kneading (see whole grain flours in Lessons, page 253). While the semi-coarse rye dough benefits from an overnight rest (the gluten strengthens), either dough is foolproof when rolled on day 1 on a nonstick surface.

WHOLE WHEAT PASTA DOUGH

As a morning person, I enjoy a head start on the day's food and prayer before sunrise

She gets up while it is still dark and prepares food for her family...

~ **Proverbs 31:15 NCV**

100% Whole Wheat Pasta Dough

For the Flour
- 3 ½ cups whole wheat flour, extra for dusting cut pasta
- 2 tsp fine grain sea salt

For the Binding Agent
- 4 eggs, room temp
- 2 Tbs olive oil
- 5 + ~2 Tbs water, room temp

Details: see whole grain flours in Lessons, page 253
- Whisk the flour and salt together in a large mixing bowl; make a well in the center
- Whisk the eggs, olive oil, and 5 Tbs of water together in a separate bowl
- Add the egg mixture to the middle of the flour well; stir with a wooden spoon until the most of the flour is incorporated as very large crumbles of dough
- Add ~1 - 2 Tbs water to form a smooth, yet very slightly dry, dough ball; this is accomplished by firmly kneading the mixture in the bowl until the flour disappears
- Transfer the dough to a nonstick surface; knead it firmly, but slowly, for ~4 min; cover; let it rest for ~5 min; knead ~1 min; cover; let it rest 30 min at room temp
- Flatten the dough on a nonstick surface; divide it into 8 equal pieces, and cover
- Roll the dough with a rolling pin, pasta roller machine, or stand mixer attachment
- For an attachment (easiest method), flatten a section of dough into a ~1/8" thick rectangle; roll it through thickest setting (1) on speed 2; fold it in thirds like an envelope and press firmly; roll it through setting (1) again by feeding the open seam edge in first; now roll the sheet through settings 2, 3, then 5, and finally 7
- Cut long sheets in half; lightly dust each side with flour; dry in a single layer while rolling other sections to aid in separation; cut into angel hair or linguini with the attachment; coil into nests lightly dusted with flour; cook, refrigerate, or freeze
- Add fresh or frozen pasta to salted boiling water; reduce the heat to med-high; boil for ~4 min; drain and toss with Bolognese or Pesto (pages 86 and 222)

NOTE: After many experiments with 100 % whole wheat pasta dough (store bought or freshly milled hard red wheat); I have found that: Tough Kneading = Easy Rolling or Easy Now = Sticky Later. While the initial dough may seem very dry, the 30 – 60 min rest transforms it into perfectly supple dough (due to the gluten development and wheat hydration). Overly hydrated dough will stick to the rollers and itself. The exact amount of water (5 – 7 Tbs total) depends on the size of the eggs and the fineness of the flour. Dusting cut pasta with flour prevents clumping during storage and cooking.

WHOLE WHEAT TORTILLAS

whole wheat pastry

whole wheat

white wheat

Experiment: Make these tortillas with whole wheat, whole wheat pastry, and white whole wheat flours. Compare elasticity and gluten formation (page 94) while kneading.

100 % whole wheat puffs up beautifully

Whole Wheat Soft Taco Shells

For the Tortillas (makes eight, 8 – 10" diameter, soft shells)
- 2 cups whole wheat flour
- ¼ cup packed coconut oil
- 1 ½ tsp salt
- ¾ cup water, very hot

Details: see whole grain flours in Lessons, page 253
- Mix the flour and salt in a large bowl with your hands; add the coconut oil in small chunks; squeeze it into the flour with your hand until a crumbly texture results
- Heat the water in the microwave for 1 min; add it to the flour mixture; swirl it, and carefully work it in with your hand (it is hot) to form a very soft, resilient dough until it pulls away from the sides of the bowl; the dough will stick less as the water cools and the oil comes to the surface; scrape the bowl and your hand clean
- Transfer the dough to a nonstick surface; knead it for ~ 2 min; divide the dough into 8 equal sized pieces; roll each into a ball; transfer them all to a bowl (their oil will prevent clumping); cover, and let them rest for at least 30 min at room temp
- Remove 1 – 2 dough balls at a time to roll just before cooking; flatten each into a mini disc, and roll into a thin circle, ~ 1/16", with a rolling pin on a nonstick surface
- Preheat an ungreased nonstick or cast iron pan over med heat for several min
- Cook tortillas ~ 1 min until bubbles form; flip them over; cook another ~ 1 min until lightly browned; reduce heat to med-low as needed to prevent over browning
- Use, or store in a Tupperware in the fridge; reheat in the microwave ~ 13 sec

NOTE: My Dad's friend Chino, who has made tortillas his entire life, taught me that the key to easy-to-roll, tender tortillas is to use a solid form of fat (lard or shortening). Coconut oil is among the healthiest of saturated (solid) fats. It is not hydrogenated, has 0g trans fat or cholesterol, and contains medium chain triglycerides (MCTs), known to boost energy and may have therapeutic effects on the brain. The MCT, lauric acid, is also known to kill bacteria, fungi, and viruses. 'Refined coconut oil' (expeller pressed) has a neutral flavor and can withstand cooking at high heat. 'Unrefined' adds a subtle coconut flavor, and is best for cooking at lower temperatures. Either can be used here. After much experimentation with flour; whole wheat, white whole wheat, whole wheat pastry or all-purpose white each work here, with equally tender and delicious results. The higher protein (more gluten) tortillas hold up to fajita sauce better and puff more. Heating the water precooks the flour, which palpably enhances the flavor and texture.

TRITICALE SOFT PRETZELS

Shaping Pretzels: cross the ends of the rope into a ribbon, flip the loop horizontally, then flip it vertically; secure the rope ends under or over the bottom; press to seal.

Caraway Seeds & Triticale are Perfect for Soft Pretzels & Mustard

Triticale Caraway Soft Pretzels

For the Soaked Flour (soak at least 30 min, up to a few hr, at room temp)

- 2 ¾ cups whole wheat flour
- 1 Tbs barley malt syrup*
- 1 Tbs olive oil
- 2 cups water

For the Dough (see whole grain flours in Lessons, page 253)

- 2 ½ cups triticale flour*
- 2 tsp sea salt
- 2 tsp instant yeast
- 2 Tbs caraway seeds

For the Water Bath

- 12 cups water
- 3 Tbs of baking soda

For the Topping: 1 egg beaten with 1 Tbs water, and flaked sea salt

Details: Preheat oven to 450 °C (bake) once dough has risen

- Mix the 4 Soaked Flour ingredients together; cover; soak for at least 30 min
- Whisk the triticale flour, salt, yeast, and caraway seeds in a large mixing bowl; add the Soaked Flour; incorporate all of the dry flour into the soaked flour to form a rough dough ball; do this by continually flipping the wet dough and pressing the dry flour into it, and kneading it in the bowl; this should take ~ 5 min total
- Transfer the rough dough ball to a nonstick surface; dust with flour, rest ~ 10 min
- Knead the dough for ~4 min; dust with flour in between turns to prevent it from sticking to your hands; form a dough ball; let it rest ~5 min; knead ~ 1 more min
- Form a dough ball, transfer it to a lightly oiled bowl; cover, let rest for ~ 1 hr 15 min until doubled in size; divide the dough into 8 pieces; roll into ~ 1" diameter ropes
- Preheat the oven to 450 °C; bring the baking soda and water to a boil
- Form the pretzels; drop 4 at a time into the baking soda bath, boil ~ 1 min to puff
- Remove pretzels with a slotted spoon; transfer to a non-stick baking sheet
- Whisk the egg and water; baste the pretzels with egg wash; top with salt
- Bake pretzels at 450 °F for ~15 min, remove from the oven; cool on a wire rack

NOTE: Rye flour results in sticky dough that requires more time to hydrate (page 94). Triticale is a rye-wheat hybrid that is easier to work with. Either works for seaming these savory pretzels. Light or home milled rye may be substituted equally for the triticale, or try dark rye (use 2 ¾ cup). Molasses may be substituted for *barley syrup.

WHOLE WHEAT POPOVERS

Popovers with Blackberry Butter Taste Even Better Than They Look

Whole Wheat Popovers with Blackberry Honey Butter

For the Popovers (makes 6 large or 12 mini popovers, or 9 muffins)
- 2 cups whole wheat flour
- ½ tsp salt
- ½ tsp baking powder
- 2 cups milk, whole or 2%
- 3 eggs

For the Blackberry Butter (blend in food processor, or whisk if using jam)
- 6 Tbs butter, room temp
- 2 Tbs honey
- 10 blackberries, or 3 Tbs jam
- ½ tsp vanilla extract

Details: Preheat oven to 450 °F (bake), reduce to 375 °F after first 10 min in oven
- Whisk the flour, salt, and baking powder together in a large mixing bowl; add the milk and eggs; whisk until the flour is incorporated and the batter is smooth
- Cover the batter; let it stand at room temp for ~ 1 hr, or in the fridge overnight
- Preheat oven to 450 °F, grease 6 wells of a nonstick popover pan (or 9 wells of a nonstick muffin pan) generously with butter; place on a sheet pan for stability
- Whisk the rested batter once more; scrape all of it into a blender
- Blend on med-high speed for ~ 2 min until bubbly and doubled in volume
- Fill each well: 6 popover (6 oz), or 9 muffin (4 oz) almost to the top with batter
- Transfer the filled wells (on the sheet pan) to the bottom third or middle rack of a 450 °F oven (with no racks above that will impede the batter from rising)
- Set a timer for 10 min; at this point the batter will have 'popped over' a few inches
- Reduce the oven temperature down to 375 °F and continue baking for 25 min
- Remove from the oven; serve warm with blackberry butter

NOTE: With a lightly crisped exterior, and tender custardy interior, these healthy popovers taste anything but. Since high protein (gluten forming) flours work best, 100% whole wheat is perfect. Of the endless 'tricks' for lofty popovers, all that is needed is: 1) room temp batter, 2) a very hot oven, 450 °F for skyscrapers, and 3) a reduced temp to prevent burning. The 1 hr rest hydrates the bran, and blending ensures a room temp, bubbly batter. An overnight hold makes for an effortless, yet impressive breakfast. Use the remaining softened butter from greasing the pan for the spread.

184

ULTIMATE WHOLE WHEAT TREATS

Favorite Whole Grain Treat: Chocolate Poeuffs

Favorite Baking Tool 'Wants': Pastry Bag Holder & Piping Bags

Favorite T-shirt from Auburn Baptist Church:
"Stand for Something or you'll Fall for Anything"

(Gluten-Free) Chocolate Poeuffs &
Maple Almond Chocolate Chip Poeuffs

These two desserts are by far the most decadent and requested recipes herein. The Chocolate Poeuffs are an adaptation of Thomas Keller's famous Bouchons. My two versions here are our favorites after extensive experimentation with flours and welcome weight gain. High quality chocolate is the essence of a spectacular Chocolate Poeuff. Try Scharffen Berger's Unsweetened Natural Cocoa Powder and Ghirardelli® 60% Cocoa Bittersweet Chocolate Chips. For the Almond Poeuffs, use pure Maple Syrup.

CHOCOLATE or MAPLE ALMOND POEUFFS

<u>For 36 Chocolate Poeuffs</u>
- 3 sticks butter, melted

Dry Ingredients
- 1 cup unsweetened cocoa
- ¾ cup sorghum flour
- ½ tsp fine sea salt

Wet Ingredients
- 3 eggs
- 1 ½ cup sugar
- 2 tsp vanilla

Dark chocolate chips, 1 ¼ cup

<u>For 36 Maple Almond Poeuffs</u>
- 3 sticks butter, melted
- ⅓ cup maple syrup, cold

Dry Ingredients
- 1 cup almond flour
- 1 ¼ cup wheat pastry flour
- ½ tsp fine sea salt

Wet Ingredients
- 3 eggs
- 1 cup sugar
- 2 tsp vanilla

Dark chocolate chips, 1 ¼ cup

Details: Preheat oven to 350 °F (bake)
- Melt the butter in the microwave for ~ 60 sec, whisk to remove lumps, reserve
    - For Almond Poeuffs, whisk the cold maple syrup into the melted butter
- Sift the Dry Ingredients together, push any clumped cocoa through to use all
    - For Almond Poeuffs, push any large almond pieces through to use all
- Add the eggs and sugar to the bowl of an electric mixer; beat on med speed for ~4 min until pale yellow; stop the mixer; add the vanilla; mix on low speed ~ 20 sec
- Add ⅓ of the dry ingredients; stir on low speed for ~ 10 sec until incorporated; add ⅓ of the wet ingredients; mix on low for ~ 10 sec; repeat twice more to use all
- For the grand finale ~ fold in bittersweet (60% or 72% cocoa) chocolate chips
- Transfer the batter to a pastry bag or Ziploc with a ~ 1 ½" diameter hole; pipe into 36 silicon bouchon wells (on sheet pans for stability), or nonstick mini muffin wells
- Bake for 12 min; remove from oven and transfer molds to a wire cooling rack
- Wait 5 min, then flip the molds over; patiently ease the Poeuffs out of the wells onto the rack by gently pinching or flicking the mold; they will slide out slowly

NOTE: While most any flour works here, gluten-free sorghum adds a hint of sweetness and a noticeable denseness to the Chocolate Poeuffs. For the Almond Poeuffs, home-milled soft white wheat adds tenderness; and chilled syrup firms the batter enough to pipe. See Resources, page 266, for bouchon molds, pastry bag holder and piping bags.

WHOLE WHEAT QUICK BREAD

But woe unto you, Pharisees! for ye tithe **mint** and rue and all manner of herbs, and pass over judgment and the love of God: these ought ye to have done, and not to leave the other undone.

~ Luke 11:42 KJV

Take heed that ye do not your alms before men, to be seen of them: otherwise ye have no reward of your Father which is in heaven. Therefore when thou doest thine alms, do not sound a trumpet before thee, as the hypocrites do in the synagogues and in the streets, that they may have glory of men.

~ Matthew 6: 1-2 KJV

Blackberry Mojito Quick Bread

For the Blackberry Mojito Bread (makes 1 standard 8 ½" x 4 ½" loaf)

- 1 stick unsalted butter
- 2 cups wheat pastry flour
- 1 cup brown sugar, packed
- 2 tsp baking powder
- ½ tsp salt
- 1 cup *blackberries, halved

- 1 Tbs fresh spearmint, minced
- zest of 1 lime, ~ 2 tsp
- ¾ cup milk, whole or 2%
- juice of 1 lime, ~ 2 Tbs
- 2 eggs, room temp
- 2 tsp vanilla extract

Details: Preheat oven to 350 °F (bake); see brown sugar in Lessons, page 253

- Melt the stick of butter; whisk, and allow to cool; grate the zest off of the lime
- Whisk the flour, sugar, baking powder, and salt together in a large mixing bowl; add the blackberries, mint, and lime zest; toss gently to distribute evenly
- Whisk the milk, lime juice, eggs, butter, and vanilla together in a separate bowl
- Add the milk mixture to the flour mixture; fold them together with a large spatula until the flour just disappears; do not over mix
- Grease a standard 8 ½" x 4 ½" loaf pan with butter
- Pour the batter into the greased loaf pan; bake for ~ 60 – 70 min until the edges are browned, and a toothpick inserted into the center comes out clean
- Transfer the pan to a wire cooling rack; cool the bread in the pan for ~ 10 min
- Run a dull knife around the edge of the pan; turn the loaf onto the rack to cool

NOTE:

The inspiration for this bread came from one of my favorite Teavana® teas, Blackberry Mojito, which is a green tea blend infused with blackberries, raspberries, and spearmint. If you are not a fan of spearmint, simply 'o-mint' it. ☺ Fresh or frozen blackberries may be used here, and frozen do not need to be dethawed. For either, cut large berries into halves or thirds. While pastry flour yields a slightly more tender cake, it can be used interchangeably with whole wheat, or whole white wheat flour. Either way, this quick bread is a healthy and delicious base for any combination of berries and citrus juice as the citric acid tenderizes the whole wheat flour. Try a traditional combination like blueberry, lemon, and poppy seed; or, let your pantry or children decide for you.

WHOLE WHEAT MINI CARROT CUPCAKES

Mini Carrot Cupcakes & Cream Cheese Icing

For the Carrot Coconut Cakes (makes ~ 6 dozen miniature cupcakes)

- 1 cup toasted chopped walnuts
- 2 cups whole wheat flour
- 2 tsp ground cinnamon
- 1 tsp grated nutmeg
- 1 Tbs baking powder
- 1 tsp salt
- 1 cup dried coconut

- 5 eggs, room temp
- 1 cup packed brown sugar
- 1 Tbs vanilla
- ½ cup organic canola oil
- ¼ cup coconut oil, melted
- 4 cups carrots, gently packed, ribbon grated

For the Icing (for 6 dozen mini cupcakes)

- 8 oz cream cheese, room temp
- 2 ½ cups powdered sugar

- 4 oz butter, room temp
- 1 tsp vanilla

Details: Preheat oven to 350 °F (bake); see brown sugar in Lessons, page 253

- Toast the walnuts on a bake pan at 350 °F for ~ 10 min; cool on a separate pan
- *Optional*, grease 3 nonstick mini muffin pans (24 wells each) with spray or butter
- Whisk the flour, cinnamon, nutmeg, baking powder, and salt together in a large mixing bowl; add the dried coconut; toss, and break up clumps if using sweetened
- Add the eggs, sugar, canola oil, coconut oil, and vanilla to an electric mixing bowl; beat on med-high for ~3 min; fold in the flour mixture, carrots, then walnuts with a large spatula; fill the muffin wells with a heaping small cookie scoop or teaspoon
- Bake ~13 min until the edges are lightly browned and a toothpick comes out clean
- Cool the muffins in the pan on a wire rack for ~ 5 min; remove to cool completely
- Icing Details: whip the butter and cream cheese in an electric mixer with the whisk to blend; add the vanilla and sugar; whip on low to combine, then high for ~ 2 min
- Pipe the icing from a pastry bag or cut Ziploc onto each cupcake and serve

NOTE: These muffins are moist, yet crunchy, and downright delicious, yet healthy. For the carrots, 8 medium yield ~ 4 cups grated. I use a Microplane® Ribbon Grater. Coconut oil may be replaced with canola, although it adds nutrition and flavor; and makes greased molds optional. Run a thin wire (like OXO's Cake Tester) around the baked edges to assist; otherwise, Bak-klene® ZT Sprays ensures failsafe removal of notoriously sticky muffins. Coconut oil can be used alone if a denser cake is desired.

Vegetables and Legumes

The one who knows that it is right to eat any kind of food must not reject the one who eats only vegetables. And the person who eats only vegetables must not think that the one who eats all foods is wrong, because God has accepted that person.

~ Romans 14:3 NCV

They brought wheat, barley, flour, roasted grain, beans, small peas, honey, milk curds, sheep, and cheese for David and his people.

~ 2 Samuel 17: 28,29 NCV

Chapter 4: For the OMNIVORES

So why do you judge your brothers or sisters in Christ?
And why do you think you are better than they are?
We will all stand before God to be judged...

~ Romans 14:10 NCV

Omnivore: An omnivore is defined as an "all-eater", based on the Latin derivations of *omni*, meaning all, and *vorare*, meaning to devour. An omnivore consumes meat or vegetation to derive its energy. While several of my friends are vegetarians, and often make an effort at veganism, even they occasionally stray from their convictions to satisfy a meat craving. We compromise on our menus, but not our friendship. While this chapter is largely for Vegetarians, I have included Tafelspitz under soups to satiate all.

- VEGETABLES
  - Convection - Chris's Mandatory Potatoes
  - Roasted - Lemon Pepper Squash Medallions
  - Sautéed - Garlic Lemon Creamed Spinach
  - Greens - Balsamic Rainbow Chard
  - Steamed – Vadouvan Vinaigrette Green Beans
  - Raw – Guacamole in a Molcajete

- LEGUMES
  - Black Turtle Beans - *That* Black Bean Salad
  - Lentils - Lentils du Puy in Paprika Tomatoes
  - Flageolet Magic Beans - Green Peppercorn & Flageolet Salad
  - Heirloom Beans - Snowcap Beans with Garlic & Almond Slivers
  - Cranberry Beans – Roman Beans with Greek Olives & Oranges

- SOUPS
  - Broth - Venison Tafelspitz
  - Decadent Cream - Cream of Morel Soup
  - Bisque - 2 x 2 Butternut Squash Bisque
  - Miso - Miso with Greens
  - Whole Grain - Ezekiel's Minestrone with Artichoke Pesto

Vegetables

My Chris *got Hoyt*. Jess's Chris *got Serious*, about Potatoes...

CONVECTION
Chris's Mandatory Potatoes

Inspiration: These potatoes are mandatory when we invite our friends Chris and Jess to dinner. Chris never fails to first call and ask, "is she making them?" then threaten, "if not, we won't show". Jess arrives embarrassed. Chris arrives "starved". Everyone leaves happy. It is now our running joke since I have served these alongside Kung Pao Venison, Venison Black Bean Chili Verde, and Mojo Venison Tortillas – to name a few. For all that the Ramrattans have done for us, the potatoes are a small price to pay.

For the Roasting Pan (see Pantry for fennel pollen, page 262)

- 2 lb of baby gold potatoes
- ½ cup olive oil
- 1 Tbs sea salt
- 20 grinds of black pepper
- 2 rosemary sprigs, stripped, leaves chopped
- 6 sprigs thyme, stripped, leaves chopped
- 2 tsp fennel pollen, or 1 Tbs fennel seeds, chopped
- 10 garlic cloves, peeled, trimmed, and minced

Details: Preheat oven to 400 °F (convection roast) or 400 °F (roast)

- Cut small potatoes in half and large potatoes into thirds, so that each piece is approximately the same size and has an exposed, skinless center
- Add the olive oil, salt, pepper, chopped rosemary and thyme leaves, fennel pollen, and minced garlic to a large mixing bowl; whisk all together
- Add the potatoes to the olive oil mixture; toss to coat all sides of the potatoes
- Transfer the potatoes and herbed oil to a ceramic or cast iron roasting pan
- Roast for ~ 35 min; flip the potatoes over with a spatula; scrape the bottom if needed to maintain their shape; roast for another ~ 10 - 20 min until golden brown

NOTE: Crispy on the outside, buttery smooth on the inside, and flavored to impress - *these* potatoes are *that* good. The convection mode truly shines here as the oven's hot circulating air crisps the potatoes to perfection. Fennel pollen is that secret ingredient that guests will inquire about. Wild, rare, tiny, golden pollen is harvested from the fennel plant just prior to blooming. Its aroma is sweet and intoxicatingly pungent. If you can find it, purchase it. If not, fennel seed imparts a near-equal intensely pleasing flavor.

ROASTED
Lemon Pepper Squash Medallions

For the Roasting Pan (see Resources for lemon pepper, page 266)
- 3 yellow squash, 1/16" coins
- 3 zucchini, 1/16" coins
- 2 Tbs olive oil
- 1 ½ Tbs lemon pepper seasoning
- ½ tsp red pepper flakes

Details: Preheat oven to 400 ° F (roast)
- Trim the ends, and slice the squash on a mandolin into very thin coins, ~ ⅛" ~ 1/16"
- Transfer the coins to a roasting pan; toss with oil, lemon pepper, and red pepper
- Roast for ~ 15 min; toss once; roast an additional ~ 5 min

NOTE: Zucchini and yellow squash, both from the squash family, are easy to grow and even easier to cook. Quickly roasting thin coins here prevents the seeds from getting soggy, which can happen with larger squash pieces. Preserved yellow lemon bits, black pepper grinds, and red pepper flakes make this dish as visually appealing as its flavor.

SAUTÉED
Garlic Lemon Creamed Spinach

For the Sauté Pan
- 1 lb fresh spinach
- 2 Tbs olive oil
- 2 garlic cloves, thinly sliced
- juice of 1 lemon
- 2 Tbs heavy cream
- ½ tsp sea salt
- 10 grinds of black pepper

Details:
- Wash the spinach, spin dry, and trim the ends (1 lb is roughly 2 fresh bunches)
- Heat the olive oil in large stockpot on high until shimmering; add the garlic, sauté for ~ 30 sec; add the spinach; sauté for ~ 2 min until tender, yet still bright green
- Stir in the lemon, cream, salt and pepper, remove from the heat, and serve

NOTE: This classic side dish is a delicious, nutrient packed alternative to steak sauce for venison. Use a very large pot to wilt the spinach, and take care not to overbrown it.

GREENS
Rainbow Chard

Balsamic Rainbow Chard

For the Rainbow Chard (see Resources for balsamic vinegar, page 266)

- 2 bunches of rainbow chard, tender portions chopped
- 2 + 2 Tbs olive oil
- 12 cremini mushrooms, halved
- 1 tsp sea salt
- 2 garlic cloves, minced
- 6 green onions; green portion, ¼" slice; white portion, minced
- 3 Tbs good balsamic vinegar
- juice of ½ lemon
- 10 grinds of black pepper

Details:

- Rinse the chard leaves; trim any damaged or tough section of the stem and discard; roughly chop the leaves and tender portions of the stem, and spin dry
- Heat 2 Tbs of the olive oil in a large stock pot on high until shimmering
- Add the mushroom halves and salt; sauté until golden and tender, ~ 5 min
- Add 2 more Tbs of olive oil; add the garlic and green onions; sauté for ~ 30 sec
- Add the chard; sauté for ~ 2 min until wilted; reduce the heat to med; cover, and allow to steam for ~ 2 min; this step will tenderize chopped stems
- Remove the cover; stir in the balsamic vinegar and lemon juice
- Allow the balsamic vinegar to reduce for ~ 1 min; remove from the heat, finish with pepper and serve

NOTE: Rainbow chard is one of three major types of Swiss chard. This leafy green is typically grown with green, red, or beautiful multi-colored (rainbow) stalks. This dark leafy green has an edible stem that is much more tender relative to kale's tough woody stem. High in vitamins A, K, and C, this super green is also packed with phytonutrients, antioxidants and B-complex vitamins including: folates, niacin, B-6 (pyridoxine), thiamin and pantothenic acid. It is also a rich source of minerals like copper, calcium, sodium, potassium, iron, manganese and phosphorus. As with wilting spinach, start with a large stockpot to allow for the significant dimensional change. Feel free to blend spinach or other greens with the chard, as shown in the top left photo. With their mild flavor, both the chard and mushrooms lend the perfect base for the green onion and garlic flavor infusion. Use the best balsamic vinegar you can find (see Pantry, page 262).

STEAMED
Vadouvan Vinaigrette Green Beans

For the Beans (see Resources for Vadouvan, page 266)

- ~1 lb of fresh green beans
- 1 tsp salt
- 20 grinds of black pepper
- 2 Tbs olive oil
- 3 Tbs white wine vinegar
- 1 Tbs Vadouvan seasoning

Details:

- Fill a medium saucepan with 2" of water; bring to a boil; add the green beans to a steaming basket and place in the water; cover and steam for ~ 7 min
- Whisk the remaining ingredients in a large bowl; add the steamed beans and toss

NOTE: You may notice that I don't bother trimming the ends of beans. I like the rustic look, and we use the stems as handles to dip the beans in the green-hued, multifaceted flavored vinaigrette. Vadouvan, a French interpretation of Masala Curry, is one of my favorite seasonings. Raw, it smells like chicken bouillon. Heated through, its aroma is complex and divine. Everyone who tries it asks what it is. If you can't find it, blend and grind a dash of each of the following dried spices together: garlic, shallots, celery seed, coriander, cumin, fenugreek, turmeric, black pepper, cardamom, and cayenne pepper.

RAW
Guacamole in a Molcajete

For the Guacamole

- 3 jalapeño peppers, deseeded, ¼" dice
- 2 garlic cloves, chopped
- 2 tsp salt

- 2 avocados, diced
- 1 tomato, diced
- juice of 1 ½ limes
- 2 Tbs cilantro leaves, minced

Details: see Pantry on molcajetes, page 262, and Lessons on peppers, page 253

- Deseed the jalapeños to taste; add the peppers and garlic to a seasoned molcajete; top with salt; grind into a coarse paste
- Add the avocados, lime juice, tomatoes, and cilantro; mash to desired smooth or coarse consistency; serve with tortilla chips, tacos, burgers, wraps, or fajitas

NOTE: A molcajete is a Mexican volcanic rock mortar and pestle that grinds guacamole into a distinctively smooth texture. If you don't have one, a food processor or blender works for a chunkier dip. Years ago, you couldn't have paid me to try guacamole. Today it is my favorite healthy indulgence. Most guacamole is made with raw onions, which I don't love. Like venison and religion, try it on your own before dismissing it.

Legumes
BLACK TURTLE BEANS

That Black Bean Salad

For the Black Beans (see Resources, page 266)

- 1 cup dried black turtle beans
- 2 bay leaves
- 1 Tbs olive oil
- 4 cups water

For the Salad

- 2 cobs sweet corn, 1 Tbs salt
- 3 tomatoes, ½" dice
- 3 jalapeño peppers, ¼" dice
- 3 chipotle peppers, minced, + 2 Tbs of its adobo sauce
- juice of 4 limes + 1 lemon
- 2 Tbs white wine vinegar
- 2 Tbs of olive oil
- ½ bunch cilantro leaves, minced
- 20 grinds of black pepper
- 5 garlic cloves, minced
- 1 tsp + 1 Tbs sea salt

Details: see Lessons on peppers and capsaicin, page 253

- Pressure cook the black beans, bay leaves, and oil in water for 25 min, then drain; or, soak the beans overnight and simmer for 1 – 2 hr; or, use canned beans
- Place the corn cobs in a saucepan; add water to 2" over the corn and 1 Tbs salt; bring to a boil; reduce heat to med-high; boil for 3 min; transfer cobs to a bowl of ice water; cool for ~ 5 min to preserve the color; drain, and slice the kernels off
- Add the cooled corn kernels, tomatoes, jalapeños, chipotles (remove membranes and seeds to taste), adobo sauce, lime and lemon juice (~ 1 cup total), vinegar, olive oil, cilantro, 1 tsp salt, and black pepper to a mixing bowl; toss and chill
- Mince the garlic cloves; add to a large mixing bowl and cover with 1 Tbs of sea salt; top with the warm drained black beans (the heat will slightly cook the garlic); toss and chill this mixture in the freezer for ~ 10 min, or in the fridge for ~ 20 min
- Add the chilled garlic black beans to the tomato salsa; toss, chill in fridge for ~ 20 min to allow the flavors to meld; serve at room temp with tortilla chips or a spoon

NOTE: If there were one recipe to make in this book, *That* Black Bean Salad would be it. Our friends ask for "that" salad again and again. Sweet, crisp corn and creamy black beans are marinated in a cilantro infused citrus juice that tones the heat from the peppers. The taste and texture of pressure-cooked black beans is incomparable, and worth the minimal effort. Fresh corn transcends this salad from good to exceptional.

LENTILS du PUY

Lentils du Puy in Paprika Tomatoes

For the Lentils du Puy (see Resources, page 266)

- 1 cup lentils du Puy (AOP)
- 4 cups chicken broth
- 7 Campari or medium tomatoes on the vine, cut in thirds
- 3 garlic cloves, thinly sliced

- 2 Tbs good smoked paprika
- ~ 2 Tbs olive oil
- ~ 2 Tbs sherry vinegar
- 1 tsp salt
- 20 grinds of fresh pepper

Details:

- Add the lentils and chicken broth to a large saucepan (round bottom if you have one); bring the mixture to a boil on high while preparing the vegetables
- Chop the tomatoes (see note) and slice the garlic cloves into very thin slivers
- Add the tomatoes, slivered garlic, and paprika to the lentils
- Once the lentils and tomatoes are boiling, reduce the heat to med; simmer uncovered for ~ 30 to 35 min to reduce the broth to a thickened gravy
- Remove from the heat, stir in the olive oil, vinegar, salt, and pepper

NOTE:

Lentils du Puy are French green lentils that differ significantly in taste and texture from standard French green lentils. Grown in Le Puy France, they are considered the caviar of lentils for good reason. They retain their gorgeous shape and color throughout the cooking process, and result in a sublimely firm rather than pasty texture. Their distinct mineral taste and lower starch content is due to the volcanic, fertilizer-free soil in which they are grown, and is unique to the protected region of Appellation d'origine contrôlée (AOC). I love all lentils; though prefer to puree those that don't hold their shape to work their naturally broken cooked texture. Rather, here, lentils du Puy are the base for a sophisticated, hybrid - stew - vinaigrette salad that could not be easier to make. Finally, the measurements here are given merely as guidelines. You may use any type and amount of fresh tomatoes that you have on hand, although, as texture is important here; I prefer to use ~ 1" chunks of coreless tomatoes that meld into the stew. Since so few ingredients are needed, use the best smoked paprika, sherry vinegar and olive oil you can find. Your desired volumes will determine either a stew or vinaigrette outcome.

FLAGEOLET MAGIC BEANS

Green Peppercorn & Flageolet Salad

For the Flageolets (see Resources, page 266)
- 1 cup flageolets, or other dried green or white bean
- 2 Tbs olive oil
- 4 cups water

For the Salad
- 2 tsp green peppercorns in brine, roughly chopped
- 2 - 3 garlic cloves, sliced thin, chopped lengthwise
- 1 tsp sea salt
- 2 Tbs olive oil
- 2 Tbs white wine vinegar
- 2 Tbs sherry vinegar

Details:
- Pressure cook the flageolets in water and olive oil for 30 min on high; drain
  - Bean cooking times vary with age; they should taste tender, not gritty or hard; re-pressurize as needed in increments of ~ 3 - 5 min until done
- Roughly chop the green peppercorns; slice the garlic into thin slivers; then cut the slivers lengthwise to form icicles, or 'garlicles'
- Add the peppercorns, 'garlicles', salt, olive oil, and both vinegars to the freshly drained, warm flageolets; the heat from the beans will slightly cook the garlic and soften the peppercorns; toss, and serve immediately warm or at room temp
- If refrigerated, reheat this bean salad gently in the microwave for ~ 20 - 30 sec

NOTE:

Flageolets are the classic light green bean used in the famous dish, Cassoulet, born in the South of France. They are perfect for bean salads as they hold both their kidney shape and beautiful pistachio-hue nicely. When properly cooked, they are firm yet creamy in texture and have a wonderfully smooth and velvety aftertaste. Our friends, Andrea and Keith Hill, love this unusual and bold combination of garlic and green peppercorns so much that they have renamed this recipe: "Magic Beans". Note that raw garlic becomes more pungent the longer it sits. You might use 3 cloves if serving immediately, or 2 if preparing a day ahead. You can substitute navy beans (which are actually a white bean); though flageolets are worth the effort to seek out or order.

HEIRLOOM BEANS

Snowcap Beans with Garlic & Almond Slivers

For the Snowcap Beans (see Resources, page 266)
- 1 cup snowcap beans, or other dried white bean
- 2 Tbs olive oil
- 4 cups water

For the Salad
- 2 garlic cloves, thinly sliced
- ½ cup slivered almonds
- 6 Tbs champagne vinegar
- 1 tsp salt
- 3 Tbs olive oil
- 15 grinds of black pepper

Details:
- Pressure cook the Snowcap beans in water and olive oil on high for 35 min; drain
  - Bean cooking times vary with age; they should taste tender, not gritty or hard; re-pressurize as needed in increments of ~ 3 - 5 min until done
- Slice the garlic into very thin slivers, for a similar appearance to the almond slivers
- Add the garlic slivers, almond slivers, champagne vinegar, salt, olive oil, and pepper to the freshly drained, warm Snowcap beans; the heat from the beans will slightly cook the garlic; toss, and serve immediately warm or at room temp
- If refrigerated, reheat this bean salad gently in the microwave for ~ 30 sec

NOTE: Snowcap beans are a beautiful heirloom bean, named after snow-crested mountains, which are famous for their beautiful colorations. Like heirloom tomatoes, certain varietals of beans, prized for a distinct feature, achieve 'heirloom' status when their seeds are passed down through a family for several generations. Snowcap beans are hearty in size, texture, and flavor. They maintain their gorgeous markings, as well as their shape when cooked, and transform into a silky smooth texture similar to potatoes; making them perfect for bean salads, soups, and chilies. Unlike lentils du Puy, which there are no substitute for, the purpose of this recipe is to get everyone excited about the many new and exciting heirloom beans available today. Paired with a great base, such as the crunchy almond and heady garlic, champagne vinaigrette here; beans are no longer boring. If you can't find Snowcaps, try this salad with Christmas Lima, Giant White Lima, European Soldier, Appaloosa, or Fava beans. With so many unique sizes, shapes, colors, textures, and flavors to choose from; the world is your bean pod.

CRANBERRY BEANS

Roman Beans with Greek Olives & Oranges

For the Cranberry Beans (see Resources, page 266)
- 1 cup Good Mother Stallard, or other red bean
- 2 Tbs olive oil
- 4 cups water

For the Dressing
- 2 garlic cloves, chopped
- 1 tsp salt
- juice of 2 lemons
- ⅓ cup white wine vinegar
- 1 - 2 tsp clover honey
- ¼ cup olive oil

For the Salad (see Pantry for olives, page 262)
- 2 oranges, peeled, wedged, and slices halved
- ¾ cup Kalamata olives, pitted
- 15 grinds of black pepper

Details:
- Pressure cook the cranberry beans in water and olive oil on high for 40 min; drain
  - Bean cooking times vary with age; they should taste tender, not gritty or hard; re-pressurize as needed in increments of ~ 3 - 5 min until done
- Add the garlic, salt, lemon juice, vinegar, and honey to a blender; blend on high for ~ 1 min to pulverize the garlic; stop the blender; slowly add the oil in a stream through the top of the blender lid, while running on med-high ~ 1 min to emulsify
- Add the orange wedges and Kalamata olives to the drained warm beans; toss with the lemon vinaigrette; serve immediately warm or at room temperature
- If refrigerated, reheat this bean salad gently in the microwave for ~ 30 sec

NOTE: Cranberry beans are also known as Borlotti or Roman beans. With their striking markings, Good Mother Stallard is one of many beautiful cranberry beans to choose from alongside Tongues of Fire, October, and Wren's Egg. Their firm yet creamy texture pairs perfectly with bold and meaty Kalamata olives. The orange wedges are the surprise ingredient here that beautifully lightens the flavor and appearance of this otherwise sultry salad. The lemon dressing ties this unexpected combination together by playing to both the sweet nutty Roman beans, and the salty Greek olives.

Soups
BROTH

Venison Tafelspitz

Inspiration: My Mother, Rosemary Guillory Hoyt, was born in Bremerhaven, Germany. Her boiled beef with root vegetables is unrivaled. This effort is in honor of her love, attention to detail, Germanic influence, and indulging my lifelong love of red meat.

For the Venison Broth Simmer

- 2 venison roasts, ~ 3 lb total
- 8 cups water
- 1 tsp peppercorns
- 1 tsp salt
- 1 head of garlic, skin on, cut in half to expose cloves

For the Root Vegetable Addition

- 1 Tbs olive oil
- 1 yellow onion, with skin on, cut in half
- 1 lb root vegetables, peeled: carrots, turnips, & parsnips
- 1 large leek, cut into 2" long pieces at a 45 degree angle
- 1 Tbs sea salt
- *Garnish* with Horseradish or horseradish aioli

Details:

- Bring 8 cups of water to a boil in a large stockpot
- Add the venison, peppercorns, salt, and garlic halves to the boiling water; allow the broth to come back to a boil; now reduce the heat to your lowest setting (low or low simmer) to achieve a very slow simmer; cover; simmer for ~ 3 hr
- Heat the olive oil in a frying pan on high; blacken the onion halves with the skin on
- Add the blackened onion, peeled root vegetables, cut leek, and salt to the broth
- Bring the stock back to a boil; reduce the heat to low; cover and simmer for ~ 1 hr
- Carefully remove the beef and vegetables; slice the beef into thick pieces
- Pour the broth into a new stockpot over a fine sieve to remove the peppercorns, onion, and garlic; press on the onion with a spoon to extract more flavor
- Arrange the venison and vegetables in bowls; top with broth or optional garnish

NOTE: In Vienna, Austria - Tafelspitz is not a soup - it is an experience. This classic Viennese dish can be eaten as a soup, or as a plate of beef and vegetables topped with a dollop of creamed or plain horseradish. Either way, you will not need a knife. This slowly boiled beef falls apart in its intensely flavored broth.

DECADENT CREAM

Cream of Morel Soup

For the Dried Morels
- 4 cups dried morels
- 4 cups water

For the Creamy Bisque
- 8 garlic cloves, minced
- 2 Tbs olive oil
- 4 Tbs butter
- 2 tsp sea salt
- reserved morel broth, above
- 2 bay leaves
- ½ cup heavy cream
- juice of ½ lemon
- 30 grinds of black pepper
- *Garnish* with lemon zest

Details:
- Bring 4 cups of water to a boil; add 4 cups of dried morels and remove from the heat; let the mushrooms hydrate for at least 20 min; mince the garlic
- Transfer the mushrooms with a slotted spoon to a cutting board; roughly chop the morels into 1/8" slices; do not discard the morel infused water
- Heat the olive oil and butter in a medium stock pot on high; add the chopped morels and sauté for ~ 4 min; reduce the heat to med
- Add the garlic and salt to the morels; sauté for ~ 30 sec to 1 min, do not burn
- Strain the reserved morel broth over a fine sieve to remove any dirt; add it to the stock pot; bring the soup to a boil; stir in the bay leaves and pepper; reduce the heat to low; cover, and simmer for ~ 30 min; remove the bay leaves
- Puree the soup until smooth, or desired consistency, using either an immersion blender directly in the pot; or transfer it to a blender in two separate batches
- Finish the soup by stirring in the heavy cream and lemon juice
- Garnish the soup with fresh lemon zest and more black pepper

NOTE:

We've got friends in high places. Since giving up a morel spot is like broadcasting a great fishing hole or treestand, I'll just dedicate this to our 'clandestine' friends. Dried morels are expensive, averaging ~ $18/ounce. Lucky for us, Chris barters fishing trips and my baked goods for them. You can substitute any 4 cup combination of dried or fresh mushrooms here. Do not soak fresh mushrooms, and use 4 cups of water total.

BISQUE

2 x 2 Butternut Squash Bisque

For the Roasted Butternut Squash
- 2 heads garlic cloves, peeled
- 2 large butternut squash, peeled, 2" cubes
- 1 Tbs sea salt
- 20 grinds of black pepper
- 2 tsp red pepper flakes
- ¼ cup water
- 3 Tbs of olive oil

For the Sautéed Leeks
- 2 Tbs olive oil + 2 Tbs butter
- 2 leeks, tender green and white parts, minced
- 2 tsp sea salt
- 4 sprigs of thyme leaves
- ¼ cup of favorite white wine

For the Grand Finale
- the squash and leeks
- 6 cups of vegetable broth
- ground black pepper
- baby chives

Details: Preheat oven to 400 °F (roast); see Lessons on deglazing, page 253
- Peel and trim the 2 heads of garlic cloves; peel and cube the squash into 2" pieces
- Add the garlic, squash, salt, pepper, red pepper flakes, water to a roasting pan; drizzle the olive oil over all; roast at 400 °F for 1 hr; stir the vegetables to loosen caramelized bits from the bottom; roast ~ 10 more min, remove from oven and cool
- Heat the olive oil and butter in a sauté pan on high until bubbling, add the leeks; sauté ~ 5 min; reduce heat to med; add salt and thyme; sauté ~ 5 min; deglaze with wine; remove from the heat to cool; add the roasted squash and garlic to the pan
- Add ⅓ of the vegetable mixture to a blender and top with 2 cups of vegetable broth; puree on high for ~ 1 – 2 min until very smooth, transfer to a stock pot
- Repeat this twice with the remaining 4 cups of broth and vegetables
- Stir and simmer all to heat through; finish with fresh ground pepper and chives

NOTE: This savory, rather than sweet, butternut bisque is the second most requested recipe herein. The 2x2 name helps me remember this simple recipe: 2 of each major ingredient, dimensionally proportioned. Use two large leeks and heads of garlic for large squash, or small for each, etc. You may be amazed at the spicy undertone that 2 tsp of red pepper flakes adds. Reduce to 1 tsp or omit if needed; and serve with bread.

MISO

For the Seaweed Salad (use wakame from miso soup, or freshly hydrated)

- 1 tsp of minced garlic, scallion, and ginger blend
- 1 tsp sesame oil
- 1 tsp low sodium soy sauce
- 2 tsp seasoned rice vinegar
- ½ tsp sesame seeds

Details:

- If you are making miso soup, blend the minced garlic, scallion, and ginger together and reserve 1 tsp for this salad; or make this mixture fresh
- Prepare the miso soup; remove the hydrated wakame with tongs, rinse with cold water, and chop into ⅛" strips; or boil wakame in water for 5 min; drain, and chop
- Toss the wakame with garlic, scallion, ginger, oil, soy, vinegar, and sesame seeds

Miso with Greens

For the Mushroom Sauté

- 3 garlic cloves, minced
- 3 green scallions, minced
- 1" piece of ginger, minced
- 1 Tbs of olive oil
- 1 tsp of chili sesame oil
- ½ tsp sea salt
- 3 shitake mushrooms, sliced very thin

For the Miso Soup (see Resources for wakame and miso, page 266)

- 4 cups water
- 2 strips of wakame
- 2 cups spinach leaves
- 10 grinds of black pepper
- 3 Tbs miso paste, try South River's Brown Barley miso

Accouterments (review sea vegetables and Pantry, pages 110 and 262)

- Seaweed Salad, recipe at left
- umeboshi paste

Details:

- Mix the minced garlic, onion, and ginger together; reserve 1 tsp for seaweed salad
- Heat the olive and chili sesame oils on high in a medium soup pot until shimmering; add the garlic, scallion, and ginger blend; sauté ~ 30 seconds; add the salt and mushrooms; sauté until the mushrooms release their juices, ~ 3 min
- Add the water, wakame, spinach, and pepper; stir and bring the soup to a boil
- Reduce the heat to low (see note); add the miso paste and stir until it dissolves
- Remove the wakame from the soup with tongs; rinse with cold water, and prepare the seaweed salad (recipe at left); serve alongside the hot miso soup

NOTE: This soup tastes and feels like pure liquid energy. Miso paste is produced by fermenting rice, barley, or soybeans with sea salt and cultured grains (koji) for as little as 5 days, or up to several years. Three major types of miso are: Shiro (sweet white), Aka (savory red or brown), and Awase (mixed). The South River Miso Company hand crafts phenomenal macrobiotics-inspired, grain infused, unpasteurized misos. Three-Year Barley is my favorite. It is a deep auburn hued, richly flavored, robustly textured miso. Never heat miso above a simmer to preserve its live probiotic microorganisms and natural digestive enzymes. Nearly any green and sea vegetable works here. Try options like savoy cabbage, bean sprouts, or bok choy coupled with wakame, kombu, or arame.

WHOLE GRAIN

Ezekiel's Minestrone with Artichoke Pesto

'Take thou also unto thee wheat, and barley, and beans, and lentiles, and millet, and fitches, and put them in one vessel, and make thee bread,' (or soup below)
~ Ezekiel 4:9 KJV

For the Grains & Beans (small beans cook with grains for the same time)
- 1 cup whole grains and small dried beans, any combination
- 2 Tbs olive oil
- 4 cups water

For the Vegetable Sauté and First Simmer
- 3 Tbs olive oil
- 2 leeks, minced
- 1 Tbs sea salt
- 4 carrots, ¼" coins
- 8 garlic cloves, minced
- 2 celery stalks, ¼" dice
- ⅓ cup of white wine
- 14 oz can diced tomatoes
- 8 cups vegetable broth
- Bouquet Garni (next page)

For the Soup and Second Simmer
- 2 ears of sweet corn kernels
- 3 kale leaves, chopped
- 4 cup water + 1 Tbs sea salt
- 1 cup dried grains and beans

Garnish: Artichoke Pesto (next page) & cooked whole wheat pasta shells

Details: refer to Whole Grains Cooking Time Table (page 106) for optional methods
- Pressure cook the grains and beans in oil and water for 25 min on high; drain
- Heat the olive oil in a large stock pot on high until shimmering; add the leeks and salt; sauté for ~ 3 min; add carrots; sauté for ~ 3 min, add garlic and celery; sauté for ~ 2 min; add the wine, tomatoes, broth, and Bouquet Garni (or ground black pepper and thyme); bring to a boil, then reduce heat to low and simmer for ~ 1 hr
- Boil the corn cobs for ~ 3 min, slice off the kernels; chop the kale leaves and discard woody stems; add the corn, kale, water, salt, and drained cooked beans and grains to the soup; simmer all for ~ 30 min; prepare the Artichoke Pesto and boil the whole wheat shells separately; add the garnishes just before serving

NOTE: Most soups taste better the second day; although this one is just as flavorful on day 1 as it is after a deep freeze. Adding cooked pasta shells separately will preserve their al dente texture; and the artichoke pesto brightens both the color and flavor.

Artichoke Pesto

For the Artichoke Pesto (garnish for soup, or dip for crackers)

- 14oz can artichokes, drained
- 2 garlic cloves, chopped
- 1 tsp sea salt
- 4 oz fresh basil leaves, stems removed
- ¼ cup walnuts
- ½ cup Parmigiano Reggiano cheese, grated
- juice of 1 lemon
- 1 Tbs white wine vinegar
- 15 grinds of black pepper
- 3 Tbs olive oil

Details: Add all of the ingredients above, except for the olive oil, to a food processor or blender; pulse until a uniform texture is achieved; with the motor running, pour the olive oil in, as a thin stream, and process for another ~ 30 sec until semi-smooth

Bouquet Garni ~ Sachets for Soup

For the Soup Sachet (see Resources for spice bags, page 266)
- 1 spice bag, tea ball, or cheesecloth and string
- 1 tsp ~ 1 Tbs peppercorns
- 2 bay leaves
- 6 sprigs of thyme
- any other desired herbs

NOTE: Slow simmered fresh herbs infuse exceptional flavor within stocks or soups. While bundles of herb sprigs can be tied together and easily removed from a soup, individual peppercorns cannot. Enter the bouquet garni, or aromatic soup sachet. This pocket full of herbs adds tremendous flavor with minimal effort at the start and finish. Add whole peppercorns, bay leaves, thyme sprigs, etc. (parsley or rosemary sprigs; sage, marjoram, or basil leaves; coriander, fennel, or celery seed; dill weed or citrus rind) to a spice bag; tie it to secure. Or, add all to a tea ball, or cheesecloth tied with string.

But the fruit of the Spirit is love, joy, peace, longsuffering, gentleness, goodness, faith, Meekness, temperance: against such there is no law. If we live in the Spirit, let us also walk in the Spirit. Let us not be desirous of vain glory, provoking one another, envying one another.

~ Galatians 5: 22, 23, 25, 26 KJV

Lo, children are an heritage of the Lord: and the fruit of the womb is his reward. As arrows are in the hand of a mighty man, so are children of the youth. Happy is the man that hath his quiver full of them.

~ Psalm 127: 3-5 KJV

Every branch in me that beareth not fruit he taketh away: and every branch that beareth fruit, he purgeth it, that it may bring forth more fruit. I am the vine, ye are the branches: He that abideth in me, and I in him, the same bringeth forth much fruit: for without me ye can do nothing. Herein is my Father glorified; that ye bear much fruit; so shall ye be my disciples. If ye keep my commandments, ye shall abide in my love; even as I have kept my Father's commandments, and abide in his love. These things I have spoken to you, that my joy might remain in you, and that your joy might be full. ...I have chosen you, and ordained you, that ye should go and bring forth fruit, and that your fruit should remain: that whatsoever ye shall ask of the Father in my name, he may give it to you.

~ John 15: 2, 5, 8, 10-11, 16 KJV

225

Chapter 5: For the Frugivores

Frugivore: A frugivore is a fruit eater, or an omnivore, who prefers fruit to other foods. I used to be the antithesis of a frugivore (see page 107). Today, after learning how to best enjoy fruit, I rarely go a day without it. Fruit juice and smoothies are the perfect way to incorporate your best, or less than perfect, bruised harvest, into your daily diet. You will enjoy nothing but a glass of pure, sweet energy, with nary a sticky finger, nor a hint of seed or soft, mealy section. Try the following diverse menu to find your favorite method and combination, and to please any -'vore' of any age.

Juicing could not be easier. Cut fruits and vegetables into ~ 1 - 2" chunks; discard only the bitter skins, rind, and large seeds, that could harm your juicer; juice, and voila! You will be rewarded with an über healthy meal or snack in < 5 min to enjoy immediately, or in a to-go cup for those en route. I transport mine in small glass bottles from lifefactory®. Use skins, seeds, and juiced pulp for composting. Or, get creative with the pulp. Use it to fortify and tenderize carrot cake muffins or other baked goods.

Smoothies, based on pulverized fruits and vegetables, are the answer to frozen fruits, especially melons, that don't defrost well. These immensely delicious, covertly healthy drinks are a high fiber, super hydrating, light alternative to a whole grain breakfast or snack any time of day. Just rinse, chop, freeze, and grind. Enjoy immediately, or in an insulated to-go cup. I carry smoothie filled, domed topped cups & straws everywhere.

- **Juicing**
  - Mango Morning
  - Blackberry Suede
  - Gingered Grapefruit Gala
  - Fuchsian Energy
  - Pineapple Partay
  - Strawberry Field of Greens

- **Frozen Smoothies**
  - Frozen Fruit & Blenders
  - Watermelon Strawberry Slushy
  - Raspberry Honeydew Slushy
  - Mango Summer Slush
  - Green Energy Smoothie
  - Electric Blue Smoothie

- **Wheatgrass**
  - The King of Greens
  - How to Grow
  - Wheatgrass Juice Bar
  - How to Juice

Juicing
Mango Morning

Sunny, Coral Colored, Caribbean Inspired Juice

For the Juice

- 1 mango, peeled, 2" dice
- ½ pint of raspberries
- 1 Bosc pear, 2" dice
- 1 lime, skin removed

Details:

- Peel the mango and slice the flesh from the pit; rinse the raspberries in a strainer
- Dice the pear with its skin on, and discard the seeds and core
- Slice the peel and rind off of the lime, and discard; quarter the lime
- Juice the mango cubes, raspberries, diced pear, and quartered lime together

NOTE: If sunshine on the beach had a taste, this might be it. As peeled mango flesh can be very slippery; you may prefer to remove the meat with the skin on, dice it on the skin, and cut the cubes away from the peel (similar to cubing an avocado).

Blackberry Suede

For the Juice
- ½ pint of blackberries
- 1" piece of ginger root
- 1 Red Anjou pear, 2" dice
- 1 lime, skin removed

Details:
- Rinse the blackberries in a strainer; slice the skin off of the ginger, and cut in half
- Dice the pear with its skin on, and discard the seeds and core
- Slice the peel and rind off of the lime, and discard; quarter the lime
- Juice the blackberries, peeled ginger, diced pear, and quartered lime together

NOTE: The Red Anjou is a sweet pear that pairs perfectly with tart blackberries and lime. Ginger elevates this juice from sweet to sophisticated. The pear skins are replete with fiber, antioxidants, and phytonutrients. If your juicer allows for pulp control, open it just slightly to reap a bit of pear skin, and a luxurious blackberry texture sans seeds.

Magenta Colored, Smooth and Sophisticated Juice

Gingered Grapefruit Gala

Ultra-Violet Colored Gingered Grapefruit Gala

For the Juice

- ½ pint of raspberries
- 1" piece of ginger root
- 1 green Bartlett pear, 2" dice
- 1 grapefruit, skin removed

Details:

- Rinse the raspberries in a strainer; slice the skin off of the ginger, and cut in half
- Dice the pear with its skin on, and discard the seeds and core
- Slice the peel and rind from the grapefruit, and discard; cube flesh into 2" pieces
- Juice the raspberries, peeled ginger, diced pear, and cubed grapefruit together

NOTE: Zingy ginger converts sour grapefruit, tart Bartlett, and sweet raspberries from breakfast to gala. Ginger is known for its anti-inflammatory, gastrointestinal, and motion sickness healing powers. Try substituting crisp Bartletts with honey-sweet, smooth Boscs, or melon-sweet, crunchy Asian pears to find your favorite green pear.

Fuchsian Energy

Shockingly Fuchsia & Delicious Beet Juice

For the Juice

- 1 large beet, 1" dice
- ½ pint of raspberries
- 1 red Bartlett pear, 2" dice
- 1 lime, skin removed

Details:

- Trim the ends off of the beet, scrub, and dice; rinse the raspberries in a strainer
- Dice the pear with its skin on, and discard the seeds and core
- Slice the peel and rind off of the lime, and discard; quarter the lime
- Juice the diced beets, raspberries, diced pear, and quartered lime together

NOTE: Earthy beets are infused with the sweetness of red pear, raspberries, and lime. Beets are rich in betanin, folate, potassium, vitamin C, and fiber. Beetroot juice offers a unique source of nitrates (typically destroyed when cooked), known to lower blood pressure and boost stamina by reducing the level of oxygen needed during exercise.

Pineapple Partay

Vivid Coral Colored Partay Juice

For the Juice

- ⅓ pineapple
- 6 strawberries
- ½ lemon

Details:

- Cut the skin off of a 2" thick pineapple slice; cut the flesh and core into 1" cubes
- Rinse the strawberries with stems in a strainer, and cut the large ones in half
- Slice the peel and rind off of ½ of a lemon and discard; quarter the peeled lemon
- Juice the pineapple flesh with core cubes, strawberries, and lemon together

NOTE: Keep the core, lose the booze, and have a partay (a party without alcohol). The taste of this juice embodies a champagne glass, yet you won't miss the bubbly. Pineapple cores contain high levels of bromelain. This protein-digesting enzyme has been used to treat inflammation, swelling, indigestion, blood clotting, and fertility.

Strawberry Field of Greens

For the Juice
- 7 strawberries, with stems
- 1 Red Anjou pear, 2" dice
- 10 turnip green leaves
- ½ lemon, skin removed

Details:
- Rinse the strawberries with stems in a strainer, and cut the large ones in half
- Dice the pear with its skin on, and discard the seeds and core
- Wash the turnip greens, and chop into 2" pieces
- Slice the peel and rind off of ½ of a lemon and discard; quarter the peeled lemon
- Juice the strawberries, diced pear, chopped turnip greens, and lemon together

NOTE: Fruit juice is the perfect vehicle for adding greens like spinach, kale, or chard to your diet. Here, mildly spicy turnip greens balances both sweet strawberries and sour lemons. Juice the strawberry stems and leaves; as they contain essential vitamins and minerals for a wide array of digestive and anti-arthritic benefits. Juicing the greens, lemons, pears, and berries, in that order, results in the lovely layers shown below.

Pink and Green Swirled Juice

Frozen Smoothies

The following smoothies are sweet, impeccably smooth, and – icy, yet never ice-y – since their base is pulverized frozen fruit, rather than ice. They taste like gourmet Italian ice, just melted to the perfect consistency, and better than the best snow cone or slushy you will ever have. With no added sugar, they are certainly the healthiest.

My first attempts at smoothies were flawless. I followed recipes that called for Häagen-Dazs sorbet, so they were not surprisingly delicious as well. While sorbet is a great base, I wanted to create fresh fruit versions from scratch. Sadly, every attempt led to under processed fruit in a sea of chunky ice. Then came the "Aha Moment". I chopped high water content fruits into blender-friendly sized chunks and froze them. This was it.

Details for Watermelon, Honeydew, and Pineapple:
- Slice the skin off of the fruit; remove cores or seeds; cut the flesh into 2" chunks
- Freeze fruit in freezer bags in a single layer (or on a pan, then transfer to a bag) to prevent ice block formation; break chunks apart in the bag for simple removal
  - Bag individual portions of one or several types to eliminate measuring later

NOTE on Liquids and Blenders: Use the recipes that follow as guidelines, rather than gospel, as your blender's volume and power will dictate the amount of liquid needed for your desired consistency. A Vitamix also includes a tamper that allows for scraping while blending, for smoothies thick enough to be eaten with a spoon. Start by measuring heaping, rather than scant, cups of frozen fruit. Process until you have a 100% uniformly colored smoothie, as dots of color indicate under processed fruit. If needed, add 2 – 4 Tbs of liquid, or scrape the sides, and process a bit more. My liquids of choice are: water, citrus juice, lemonade, and coconut water (see Pantry, page 262).

Watermelon Strawberry Slushy

Hot Pink, Thirst Quenching, Frozen Smoothie

For the Frozen Smoothie (makes 1 large, ~ 18 oz, or 2 small smoothies)
- 4 large fresh strawberries
- 1 ½ cups frozen watermelon
- ¾ cup frozen pineapple
- juice of 1 lemon
- ~ ½ cup water
- handful of spinach, *optional*

Details: (see note on Liquids and Blenders, page 233)
- Rinse the fresh strawberries, remove the stems, and halve them; add to a blender
- Top with the frozen watermelon, pineapple, lemon juice, and water
- Start the blender on slow speed until the frozen fruit begins to pulverize; ramp up to high speed for 1 - 2 min until smooth; add liquid, or scrape the sides if needed

NOTE: The watermelon-pineapple frozen base is so delicious that no sugar is needed; although, lemonade may be used as the liquid if you'd prefer to simplify prep or sweeten it a bit. Fresh blueberries or raspberries work equally well here. Try adding a handful of fresh spinach for a hint of earthy flavor, and as an introduction to green smoothies.

Raspberry Honeydew Slushy

Very Raspberry, Very Refreshing, Cool Honeydew Slushy

For the Frozen Smoothie (makes 1 large, ~ 18 oz, or 2 small smoothies)
- ½ pint fresh raspberries
- 1 ½ cups frozen watermelon
- ¾ cup frozen honeydew
- ~ ⅔ cup favorite lemonade

Details: (see note on Liquids and Blenders, page 233)
- Rinse the fresh raspberries, and add to a blender
- Top the with the frozen watermelon, honeydew, and lemonade
- Start the blender on slow speed until the frozen fruit begins to pulverize; ramp up to high speed for 1 - 2 min until smooth; add liquid, or scrape the sides if needed

NOTE: This vitamin packed, cool honeydew smoothie is super hydrating, yet intensely flavored thanks to the fresh raspberry infusion. Fruit infused, not-from-concentrate lemonades are delicious; and eliminate most of the prep work. Try Simply Limeade®, Simply Lemonade® with Raspberry (shown); or use fresh citrus juice and water.

Mango Summer Slush

For the Frozen Smoothie (makes 1 large, ~ 18 oz, or 2 small smoothies)

- ⅓ cup fresh raspberries
- 3 fresh strawberries, stemmed
- 1 cup frozen mango
- 1 cup frozen pineapple
- juice of 1 lime
- ~ ½ cup coconut water

Details: (see note on Liquids and Blenders, page 233)

- Rinse the raspberries and strawberries; halve the strawberries; add to a blender
- Top the with the frozen mango, pineapple, lime juice, and coconut water
- Start the blender on slow speed until the frozen fruit begins to pulverize; ramp up to high speed for 1 - 2 min until smooth; add liquid, or scrape the sides if needed

NOTE: Whole mangos are phenomenally delicious when in season; although unripe mangos, fresh or frozen, can have a slight chalky taste. Here, sweet berries, fresh acidic lime, and enzyme rich pineapple overcome this. Coconut water adds a hint of Caribbean flavor and is a tremendous source of nutrients, natural electrolytes, and potassium. Fresh coconut water takes this smoothie to the next level (see Pantry, page 262).

Coral Summer Cooler for Any Season

Green Energy Smoothie

Emerald Green Frozen Smoothie for Green Greenies

For the Smoothie (makes 1 large, ~ 18 oz, or 2 small smoothies)

- 1 green Bartlett pear, 1" dice
- 1 kale leaf, woody stem removed, 2" chop
- 1 ½ cups frozen honeydew
- juice of 1 lime + ~ ¼ cup water, or ~ ⅓ cup limeade

Details: (see note on Liquids and Blenders, page 233)

- Dice the pear with its skin on, and discard the seeds and core; chop the kale
- Add the pear, kale, frozen honeydew, lime, and water to a blender
- Start the blender on slow speed until the frozen fruit begins to pulverize; ramp up to high speed for 1 - 2 min until smooth; add liquid, or scrape the sides if needed

NOTE: If you are ready to try green smoothies, look no further. This is it for health and flavor. Kale may sound like a too bitter a green for newbie greenies; but here, it blends to yield a rather sweet, yet garden-fresh tasting, frozen treat.

Electric Blue Smoothie

For the Juice (makes 1 large, ~ 18 oz, or 2 small smoothies)
- 2 rainbow chard leaves
- ½ cup fresh blueberries
- 1 cup frozen honeydew
- ½ cup frozen pineapple
- juice of 1 lime + ~ ¼ cup water, or ~ ⅓ cup limeade

Details: (see note on Liquids and Blenders, page 233)
- Remove tough portions of stem from the chard; chop the leaves into 2" pieces
- Rinse the blueberries in a strainer; add the chard, blueberries, frozen honeydew, frozen pineapple, lime juice, and water to a blender
- Start the blender on slow speed until the frozen fruit begins to pulverize; ramp up to high speed for 1 - 2 min until smooth; add liquid, or scrape the sides if needed

NOTE: Oddly enough, this beautiful blueberry and vibrant chard combination results in a hint of banana flavor. Try this blend first, then other greens and berries, to explore the healthy world of green smoothies with unique and limitless flavors.

Vibrant Blue Frozen Smoothie for Advanced Greenies

Wheatgrass Juice Fountain of Youth

...All flesh is grass, and all the goodliness thereof is as of the flower of the field: The grass withereth, the flower fadeth: because the spirit of the Lord bloweth upon it: surely the people is grass.

— Isaiah 40:6,7 KJV

Wheatgrass is often called the "**King of Greens**" for its potentially miraculous powers of healing and unadulterated vitality. Many declare that it can cure cancer, reverse grey hair, prevent diabetes, treat ulcerative colitis, and assuage numerous chronic illnesses. While scientific evidence is insufficient to validate these claims, too many remarkable accounts exist to ignore its possibilities. Review Ann Wigmore's, *The Wheatgrass Book,* and try it for a month to form your own opinion. Wheatgrass juice is a concentrated elixir of vitamins, minerals, enzymes, and chlorophyll, the green biomolecule known for fueling photosynthesis and its powers of purification. You can easily **grow your own**. Soak 1 cup of wheat kernels in water for ~ 12 hr. Drain and rest ~ 18 hr; rinse every ~6 hr. Spread a thin layer of sprouted wheat over 2" of topsoil. Cover with paper towels; mist with water for 2 days. Remove towels; expose it to sunlight; water daily, ~ 7 ~ 10 days.

Wheatgrass Shooters & Juice Bar

For the Wheatgrass Juice Blends, from Left to Right
- ~ 1 cup wheatgrass, 1 lime, ½ pint blackberries, and 1 red Anjou pear
- ~ 1 cup wheatgrass, 1 lemon, and 4 ~ 6 strawberries with their stems
- ~ 1 cup wheatgrass and ½ lemon
- ~ 1 cup wheatgrass, 1 orange, and 1 Bartlett pear

Details: a slow masticating juicer works best here, see Resources, page 266
- Cut fresh blades of wheatgrass at their base, 5" or taller, after 7 days of growth
- Remove peel and rind from citrus fruit; remove seeded cores from pears
- Chop wheatgrass blades into 1" pieces; juice with suggested combinations above

NOTE: Wheatgrass juice, on its own, has an assertively grassy flavor, tart undertones, and a lingering, bittersweet aftertaste. While considered an acquired taste, some love its essence in the purest form. We enjoy it best when simply blended with a citrus fruit and a few berries, which cuts the sharpness and highlights its lovely tang. For those new to wheatgrass, add a handful to your favorite juice blend to mute its domineering flavor.

Sweet Rewards for Hard Work

Chris is more than 30' high in this tree.

This year, we hung 8 fixed treestands, and 2 ladder stands, in 1 very long weekend.

Hunting is hard work made enjoyable by time together.

Some folks think hunters are lazy. I know from personal experience that it is a year round job, which starts early and ends late, yet is unequivocally gratifying.

Chapter 6: Sweet Hearts & Preview

- **Sweet Treats**
    - o Bubble Gum Gelato
    - o Chai Tea Latté Macarons
    - o Royal Gingerbread Whitetails

Farmers raise cattle. Chris and I raise and eat wild venison. We spent the past two summers developing food plots for whitetail on nights and weekends. Without a plow, this involves mowing, disking, and then dragging a harrow. Next, acres of dried grass must be hand raked, carried to a wheel barrel, and moved off of the plot to prepare a good seed bed. This land is limed, planted, fertilized, and groomed once more by hand. Then, we hike up steep mountainsides with heavy treestands, climb tall trees, install all of the stands, and finally, trim out shooting lanes with pole saws.

While typing in the woods during breaks, I deliberated on adding desserts to a largely healthy cookbook. After two 14 hr days, I deemed farming and hunting worthy of a few sweet treats. They may even motivate you to up your own exercise regime.

The following egg-based desserts are a preview into the next book, which will focus on wild, farm-raised, or commercial fowl: chicken, turkey, duck, grouse, doves, quail, and pheasant. Venison, gelato, macarons, and above all, faith, will be recapped.

I hope you have enjoyed *Hunt & Gather* so far. ~ Jen Lalli

Bubble Gum Gelato

Inspiration: My husband and I have a few unique childhood things in common. First, we are both left-handed; though we write with our right hands. Second, our all-time favorite ice cream flavor is Bubble Gum. Chris has asked me to try to make it for years. As bubble gum flavoring was difficult to find, I gave up on the idea. Recently, I began making gelato steeped with natural flavors, and tried this method with bubble gum (using Bazooka Squares and Nuggets, Dubble Bubble, or French Malabar® Cotton Candy gums). To our delight, it worked. We like this grown-up gelato version even better.

Thermal Conductivity (κ) of Serveware: Ceramic dishes and metal spoons melt ice cream too quickly. If you have ever wondered why, refer back to our old friends: κ and heat capacity (C_p) (see page 29). Average κ for polymers, ceramics, and metals are respectively 0.10, 10, and 200 W/m·K. Average C_p for polymers, metals, and ceramics are 1600, 800, and 450 J/kg·K. This means that it takes a polymer bowl twice the energy (C_p), of a ceramic dish, to absorb the heat from your hands or the environment. Further, polymers are an order of magnitude worse than ceramic at transferring this heat (κ) to the gelato. Serve gelato in silicon bowls or waxed paper cups for perfection.

Bubble Gum Gelato

For the Gelato
- 2 cups whole milk
- 1 cup heavy cream
- 10 pieces of bubble gum, chopped in half

- ⅓ + ⅓ cups of sugar
- 5 egg yolks
- ¼ cup bubble gum pieces, nuggets or chopped squares

Details: a thermometer and high κ Cu saucepan, page 29, are optimal here
- Add the milk, cream, bubble gum, and ⅓ cup of sugar to a saucepan; dissolve the sugar over med heat and stir to prevent a skin from forming until small bubbles form at the edges (at 170 °F); remove from heat; cover to steep for at least 20 min
- Pour the gum infused cream over a strainer into a second bowl; discard the gum; if it sticks to the strainer, it can be removed by hardening in ice cold water
- Separate the yolks from 5 eggs; save 4 egg whites in a Tupperware for macarons
- Add the 5 egg yolks and ⅓ cup of sugar to a mixing bowl; whisk until pale yellow
- Return the strained cream to the saucepan, and reheat to 170 °F
- Transfer one ladle of hot cream to the egg yolk mixture and whisk; repeat this until half of the cream has been added; now, add the tempered (warmed) egg yolks to the cream in the saucepan (tempering yolks prevents scrambled eggs)
- Heat on med-low (to 185 °F) until the cream transforms into a custard that holds a line drawn down the back of a wooden spoon; do not boil; stir gently for ~ 10 min to prevent thickening on the bottom of the pan and to help steam escape
- Pour the custard into a bowl over a strainer; fill a large bowl half way with water and ice; nestle the custard bowl in the ice bath; cool the custard to room temp
- Remove the custard bowl from the ice bath; cover, and refrigerate overnight
- Churn gelato in an ice cream machine; add gum nuggets during last 5 min of cycle

NOTE: Gelato is made with more eggs and less cream than ice cream; making it a lower fat, intensely flavored treat. Authentic gelato is also denser as it is typically mixed at a lower speed to minimize air incorporation. Both ice cream and gelato can become too firm once frozen. To revive the velvety, rather than melted, texture of freshly spun gelato, stir it in a silicone bowl or waxed paper cup with a plastic spoon. If you are not feeling like a kid, steep a vanilla bean rather than gum, and omit the bubble gum nuggets.

French Macarons

After making gelato, try something fun with the reserved egg whites...
Cardamom Perfumed French Macarons with Black Tea Buttercream

For the Black Tea Buttercream (to fill > 24 Macaron Sandwich Cookies)

- 4 Tbs butter, melt in sauce pan
- 4 tsp tea leaves, or from 2 bags
- 4 oz cream cheese, cold, cubed
- 1 tsp favorite honey
- 1 tsp vanilla bean paste
- 1 ½ cups powdered sugar

Details: (steep your favorite loose black tea in melted butter over very low heat, 5 min)

- Pour tea infused butter over a strainer; press on leaves to extract; discard leaves
- Add the black tea butter, cream cheese, honey, and vanilla to an electric mixing bowl; blend on low speed with whisk; add sugar; whip on high for 1 min until fluffy
- Transfer the icing to a pastry bag with a ~ ½" opening; pipe onto the flat sides of half of the cooled macarons; top with the remaining macarons to form sandwiches

NOTE: My friend, Michelle's daughter, Elizabeth Berg, once asked if we made "tiny hamburgers" at NanoSonic. It seems neither nanotechnology, nor French delicacy, are safe from this descriptor - regardless of the their sophistication and intricacy.

Vanilla Chai Latté Macarons

Inspiration: My Mom's sister, Aunt Petra, suggested I try a vanilla chai latté rather than my usual espresso drink on a jaunt to our local bookstore. Infused with cardamom, vanilla, ginger, and cinnamon; they are delicious. Aunt Pet also introduced me to the world of Christian literature that day.

For the Macarons, ~48 shells: use measured or (weighed amounts)

- ~ 1 ½ cup almond flour (160 g)
- ~ 1 ¼ cup powdered sugar (160 g)
- 1 tsp ground ginger
- 2 tsp ground cardamom, or ~20 pods (see Pantry, page 262)
- ½ tsp Saigon cinnamon
- 3 XL egg whites (115 g), room temp
- ⅛ tsp cream of tartar
- ½ cup granulated sugar (100 g)
- seeds from 1 bean, or 1 tsp vanilla

Details: preheat oven to 325 º F (bake) while the macarons are drying at room temp

- Add the almond flour, powdered sugar, ginger, cardamom, and cinnamon to a food processor; pulse to pulverize ~ 1 min; sift this mixture; push with your hand to use as much as possible; discard particles (~ 2 Tbs) too large to pass through
- Add the egg whites to a dry electric mixing bowl; beat on speed 6 for 30 sec with whisk; stop mixer; add cream of tartar; beat 30 sec; add granulated sugar; reduce speed to 4; beat for 7 min; stop mixer; add the vanilla; increase speed to 8; beat for ~ 1 - 3 min to a glossy meringue that holds a stiff peak; check every 30 sec
- Fold the almond mixture into the egg whites with a large spatula; stop folding when the batter flows like lava as a thick ribbon from the spatula, yet thin enough for piped tips to flatten; transfer batter to a pastry bag with a ~ ½" opening
- Line 3 insulated (or double layer) cookie sheets with Silpats or parchment paper
- Pipe the batter to form ~ 16 - 18 macarons per sheet, each being ~ 2" in diameter
- Hold the pan with one hand, and tap gently underneath with the other hand to help flatten piped tips and remove large air bubbles; if the tips don't smooth on their own within 1 min, use barely wetted fingertips to lightly smooth the tips flat; or, flatten tips by decorating with a central candied flower, sprinkles, or dragées
- Let macarons sit for 15 – 45 min until dry to the touch (up to 1 hr for wetted tips)
- Bake in oven for ~ 12 min; watch the pretty ruffly bubbled macaron "feet" grow
- Cool on Silpat (off of pan) for 2 min; transfer to a wire rack; cool, and fill shells

NOTE: Macaron texture is optimal after "maturing" in the fridge overnight, or freezing

A Well-Unplanned Trip to
La Maison Ladurée & La Cuisine Paris

I asked My Mom, Mother-in-Law, and Sister-in-Law if they would go to
Paris with me to Taste Some Cookies...

Macarons, perhaps the epitome of picturesque French confections, are based on just 4 ingredients: egg whites, almond flour, powdered, and granulated sugar. While typical recipes infer innocent simplicity, famous pastry chefs worldwide concede that macarons are one tough cookie to perfect. Their charm, infinite palette of beautiful hues, and limitless flavor combinations, ultimately overshadow challenges with an irresistible allure. An aesthetically "perfect" macaron has: a shiny, smooth, domed top (free of cracks or crumbles), a flat bottom (not sticky or hollow), encircled by a high ruffled skirt (known as the foot, or "pied"), and a layer of the creator's filling aligned with the edges of both feet. Textural elements include an air-like crisp shell with a melt-in-your mouth center.

The macaron recipe given here is my creative culmination of - 1 of at least 50 batches - based on systematic variations of self-engineered recipes and from 7 different books. Note that this was for only 1 of the 3 major methods (French, versus Italian and Swiss). Successful batches were not reproducible. Failures were a comical, yet tasty mix of cracked, hollow, sticky, and even exploded cookies. **Obsessed**, I began studying **cookbooks in my hunting blind**. Next, I made a spreadsheet to distinguish ratios of sugars/egg white/almond flour; as well as skin formation time, tapping verses banging the pan to remove bubbles, oven temperature, oven mode, and whether the door should remain opened or closed while baking. Finally, I found that the egg white beating technique was ultimately paramount for success or failure. This makes sense since macarons are meringues! You'd think a chemist would have realized that earlier.

I made a batch of beautiful pistachio green macarons for a New Year's Eve party for our friend Lee, President of Greenhouse Boardshop (see the following pages for macaron photos and equipment). His friend Brooke was amused that someone brought macarons since he used to work for *the* Thomas Keller. While Brooke told me that my macarons looked and tasted authentic, I had to be sure. I tried many local and online sources, though textures and taste varied. Then, I found the originator: **La Maison Ladurée**. At the time, they did not deliver to the United States.

I decided it was time for a taste of Paris after 10 years of dreaming. I booked a 4-day trip, and made no plans beyond a 2 hr **macaron class** at **La Cuisine Paris** and lunch at Ladurée teahouses. Kathy, Laurel, and Rose were in charge of historic sites, though we all agreed that our long lunches and laughter together in class were what we enjoyed most. We not only found that the macarons herein are indeed on par with Paris, but we will also forever treasure the impromptu idea that resulted in a dream come true.

Green Macaron Batter, Chai Shells in Oven, Black Tea Buttercream Filling

Pastry Bag Holders, Bags, and Jumbo Tips make Piping Batter and Icing Effortless

Anastasia Macarons with Real Chocolate Sprinkles: Drying and 'Pied'ing

Anastasia Macarons are Plain Vanilla – Omit the Spices and Black Tea

Whole Wheat Whitetails

My Helpers, Caitlin & Matthew, Decking the Deer

For the Royal Icing (decorates 4 discs of baked gingerbread cookies)

- 3 egg whites, room temp
- ¼ tsp cream of tartar
- 4 cups powdered sugar
- 1 tsp vanilla
- food coloring
- silver dragées, *optional*

Details:

- Add the egg whites to a dry electric mixing bowl; beat on med speed with whisk until foamy, ~ 30 sec; add the cream of tartar, beat ~ 30 sec; stop the mixer; add the powdered sugar; beat on low speed until the sugar is incorporated; scrape the sides; beat on high speed ~ 2 min until glossy; add the vanilla; beat ~ 20 sec
- Divide and transfer the royal icing into separate bowls for each desired color
- Mix a few drops of food coloring into each bowl until desired colors are achieved
- Transfer each icing color to separate pastry bags, fitted with decorating tips, or a Ziploc bag with a small hole cut at the corner; pipe the icing (see next page), and allow it to dry; store iced cookies in Tupperware or cookie jars

Royal Gingerbread Whitetails

For the Gingerbread Cookies (4 discs of dough, ~ 40 – 48 cookies):

- 1 cup butter, softened
- 1 cup brown sugar, firmly packed
- 1 cup molasses
- 1 tsp fine sea salt
- 1 Tbs vanilla
- 1 egg

- 4 ½ cups whole wheat flour
- 1 Tbs ground ginger
- 1 Tbs unsweetened cocoa
- 1 tsp Vietnamese cinnamon
- 1 tsp fresh ground nutmeg
- 1 tsp baking soda

Details: preheat oven to 350 °F (bake), see sugars & flours in Lessons, page 253

- Add the butter and brown sugar to an electric mixing bowl; mix on med-high speed with paddle for ~ 4 min until the sugar is dissolved into the butter
- Scrape the butter down from the sides; add the molasses, salt, and vanilla; mix on med speed ~ 1 min; scrape down the sides, add the egg; mix on low speed ~ 1 min
- Whisk the flour, ginger, cocoa, cinnamon, nutmeg, and baking soda together
- Add half of the flour blend to the butter mixture; mix on low speed until the flour is absorbed; remove the bowl from the mixer and scrape the paddle clean; add the remaining flour; mix gently with a wooden spoon until the flour disappears
- Allow the flour to hydrate by sitting for ~ 10 min; transfer to a nonstick surface; fold the dough gently a few times to ensure the flour is incorporated; form 4 discs, ~ ½" thick; wrap each in saran wrap; refrigerate for at least 4 hr (or freeze)
- Remove one disc at a time from fridge to keep others chilled; transfer a disc to a floured nonstick surface (Silpat is best); roll the dough between the nonstick surface and saran wrap to ~ ¼" thick; adjust saran between each roll to help it stretch; sprinkle flour below the dough as needed (flour eases transfer)
- Cut out shapes; transfer cut-outs to a nonstick baking sheet
- Repeat with other discs on a floured surface; reroll leftover dough up to 3 times
- Bake for 6 min; remove from oven; allow cookies to cool first on the pan for 6 min; then, transfer cookies directly to a wire rack to cool completely
- Pipe a thin outline of Royal Icing (recipe at left) around the perimeter of each cookie; pipe borders, and fill them in with colors to decorate; top with dragées (edible metallic confection), colored sugar, sprinkles, or real chocolate sprinkles

NOTE: Gingerbread cookies are a great gift and the color is perfect for whitetails.

Chapter 7: Lessons Learned

In the Kitchen

You Don't Learn by Being Perfect: Mistakes often lead to discoveries.

Deglaze Roasted & Pan Seared Food: Tremendous flavor can be extracted from the caramelized bits of seared dishes (meat, fruit, or vegetables). Hold off on washing the pan, even when the browned bits look burned. Flavorful pan sauces are made by quickly dissolving the bits into a hot liquid. Remove roasted food from the pan, heat the pan on high on the stovetop, add liquid, scrape the pan, stir to incorporate, and boil until your desired concentration is reached. My deglazing liquids of choice include wine, champagne, beer, other spirits, vinegar, cider, fruit juice, broth, or butter. The recipes herein call for < 1 cup of wine to deglaze; and most of the alcohol boils off within minutes.

Don't Forget the Oven Mitt when Deglazing Pan a Roasted Sauce: After removing the pan from the oven, the handle is searing hot. You may instinctively grab the handle now that it is on the stovetop, without a mitt, to steady it while scraping the browned bits. If you burn yourself once this way, you will probably never do it again.

 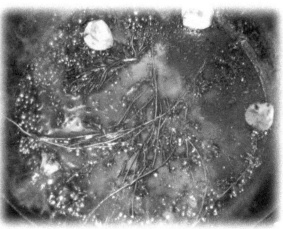

Pepper Membranes and Seeds Add Spice – Capsaicin can Burn Skin: Capsaicin, the main capsaicinoid in chili peppers, is the source of spice in your hot wings and the burned fingertips they may leave you with. First isolated in the 19th century, it was later used as a topical anesthetic for the numbing sensation it imparts on skin. Concentrated levels of capsaicin are found in the membranes and seeds of peppers; thus many recipes herein remind you to deseed and remove membranes to your taste. Since capsaicin is a hydrophobic (water repelling) wax; oil-dissolving reagents work best to remove it from your skin. Try oil-stripping dish detergents or automotive soaps. Or, rub with alcohol (any type) and then wash with soap. Do not touch your eyes until you are certain all remnants are gone. Preventing contact is the safest method to avoid this mimicked chemical burn. Wear disposable or cut resistant, washable gloves, especially if you have dry or cracked hands, which readily absorb and hold oils.

Invest in a Multifunctional Cut Resistant Glove: I wear a Microplane® glove to prevent capsaicin burns. It works great, and it rinses and dries quickly. I should have worn it for its intended purpose, to protect hands while chopping, grating, or using a mandoline for paper-thin slicing. I was grating soft cheese in a rush, pushing vertically with significant force, instead of gently at a safer horizontal angle. A wide ribbon blade cut half way through my nail bed and nearly removed the tip of my thumb. ☹

Someone is Almost Always Worse off than You: We had a few friends over for dinner the evening of the thumb massacre. I whined about how we almost cancelled due to my "boo-boo" (covered with a Pink Camouflage band-aid); and feared that I might permanently lose the feeling in my thumb. Our friend Lee, who runs Winkle's Dairy Farm, said, "I believe you will regain feeling - look – I cut my thumb clean off; they sewed it back on, and I have feeling today". My thumb was numb and ashamed. Lee said that very few dairy farmers have all of their limbs or digits. It is difficult and dangerous work. Thank your dairy farmers in prayer before your next bowl of ice cream!

Organize Complex Recipes in Batches:

Organize recipes with long lists of ingredients into batches to prevent forgetting anything. Each batch should include items with similar cooking times, which can thus be added at the same time. For example, the Venison Loin Black Bean Chili Verde recipe herein suggests preparing a Green Pepper Bowl and a
Tomatillos Bowl (shown at right). I also prep a Venison Bowl by simply tossing the meat with salt and pepper, as it is easy to forget to add salt and pepper while searing.

There are no Recipe Police: If you don't have enough of an ingredient or don't think you will like what is called for, substitute roughly the same amount of your chosen item. I prefer to cook with leeks, scallions (green onions), and garlic rather than onions. Replace each leek, head of garlic, or bunch of green onions with one onion if desired.

Baking Police Patrol: Ingredient ratios, cooking times, and temperatures matter.

Trust the Whole Grain Flour Recipes: Whole grain flours are not difficult to work with. They just behave a bit differently from the all-purpose white flours we are use to. Home milled and commercial whole grain flours contain ground bran and germ in addition to the endosperm, thus their textures vary according to grind size. Larger particulate inclusions require a bit more liquid and or time to fully hydrate. Thus, doughs that initially feel sticky are typically perfect after the recommended resting (hydration) time.

Trust your Instincts on Timing: The venison recipes in this book recommend medium-rare cooking times. With experience and coordinated meals, you may not need timers or thermometers. When pan searing or grilling, meat is typically ready to flip once it releases from the pan after a vigorous shake, or a gentle prod with the spatula.

Use Pour Spouts for Cooking Oils: I use liquor bottles to dispense cooking oils that I frequently use, as they accommodate pour spouts perfectly. I traded Courvoisier for olive oil since the navy color matches my kitchen. Similarly, a Canadian whiskey bottle boasting a deer head now holds peanut oil. If you want to try this with vinegar, the spouts must be closed to avoid fruit flies.

Prevent Brown Sugar Bricks: Never run to the store again in desperation after finding a brick of old brown sugar. For immediate revival: microwave the amount needed in a bowl covered with a damp paper towel for 20 sec increments until hydrated. For long-term recovery: place a wet paper towel in a tiny bowl within a sealed container overnight. Remove the towel and bowl; and the sugar will remain hydrated for months. Since brown sugar has a higher moisture content than white sugar, it results in baked goods that are more moist than crisp. Use an equal amount in place of, or combined with, white sugar as desired.

Don't be Afraid to Burn Food: Heat cooks food, period. Turn up the heat to high when searing; allow food to splatter and hiss. Searing meats and vegetables not only caramelizes them; it also forms a force field that traps moisture in. One exception is minced garlic. It can withstand heat for extended times when sautéed with other ingredients; though it burns to a bitter unpalatable crisp when sautéed alone in < 1 min.

Don't be Afraid to Get your Hands and Kitchen Dirty: It is important to stay organized and wipe countertops during every step possible; although organization should not equate debilitation. Don't be afraid to let grease splatter, see the flour fly, or let the lemon juice hit the counter. You can replace things, but not your sanity. We were cautioned against marble countertops due to its fragility. I reasoned that it was used in kitchens centuries ago where it still stands and looks great. We guard it as best we can, and try to view mistakes as memories.

Ultra-Thick Smoothies: I used 4 blenders with pitcher sizes ranging from 32 - 64 oz (2 without tampers) to make the smoothies herein. A tamper removes air pockets from ultra thick blends by mixing from the top, and has a fixed length that won't hit the blade. You can improvise with a spatula as shown. Just be sure to stop the motor while pushing on the mixture.

Don't Judge your Sous-chefs, or Anyone: Next time a loved one or even a chef overcooks the game, wilts the green beans, or knocks over the cake; pause before you speak. Is any meal worth hurting someone's feelings? Food is a thing. Love is priceless.

Lessons Learned

In Life

God Puts All Pain to Use

You may learn something every time you are hurt in the kitchen or life

God Will Never Give You More Than You Can Handle

He will never abandon you, even if that's what you think you want

God Has Perfect Timing

He knows what is best and when it is best, and makes time for the things that matter

Listening to the Holy Spirit can Bring Peace on Earth

Have you ever heard someone tell you to "listen to your inner voice", yet you can't hear anything? It might be time to take a step back and look at your life's direction from someone else's perspective, perhaps the Holy Spirit's viewpoint. If you have ever caught yourself questioning a negative statement that you are about to make, an e-mail you are about to send, or an ingredient you are about to use – this is probably the Holy Spirit telling you, "not so fast, don't do it!" *This* is that inner voice. If you can hear it during the potential negative decisions, start listening for it to make game changing positive decisions. Start asking yourself what you can do to:

brighten someone else's day

solve a problem that could help your household or the world

listen more carefully to others

respond compassionately to others

help someone that you don't know; or better yet, who doesn't like you

make someone laugh or cry tears of joy

not hurt someone's feelings

not feel guilty about past decisions

not second guess yourself today

not go to bed dwelling or doubting

not to worry; but rather have faith in God's plan for you

There are different kinds of gifts, but they are all from the same Spirit. There are different ways to serve but the same Lord to serve. And there are different ways that God works through people but the same God. God works in all of us in everything we do. Something from the Spirit can be seen in each person, for the common good. The Spirit gives one person the ability to speak with wisdom, and the same Spirit gives another the ability to speak with knowledge. The same Spirit gives faith to one person. And, to another, that one Spirit gives gifts of healing. The Spirit gives to another person the power to do miracles, to another the ability to prophesy. And he gives to another the ability to know the difference between good and evil spirits. The Spirit gives one person the ability to speak in different kinds of languages and to another the ability to interpret those languages. One Spirit, the same Spirit, does all these things, and the Spirit decides what to give each person.

~ Corinthians 12:4-11 NCV

But the truly happy people are those who carefully study God's perfect law that makes people free, and they continue to study it. They do not forget what they heard, but they obey what God's teaching says. Those who do this will be made happy.

~ James 1:25 NCV

Trust the Lord with all your heart, and don't depend on your own understanding. Remember the Lord in all you do, and he will give you success.

~ Proverbs 3:5,6 NCV

"When God blesses you, He rarely has you in mind".

~ Pastor E. V. Hill

Lessons Learned

In the Field

Respect the Outdoors and Others' Interests

I knew just enough about fly fishing before I met Chris to enjoy our first few dates, streamside, with fly rods and picnic baskets in tow. At the time, I didn't realize how deep his love for the outdoors was, or that he would become obsessed with hunting permit on the fly and bow hunting mature bucks. As we later fished local fresh and exotic salt waters (Belize, Cat Island, and Eleuthera); I came to love our time on the water together. The glistening waters along mountainous terrain and sun-soaked crystal clear flats were mesmerizing. Hunting, however, was a complete enigma to me. I could not understand why anyone would want to spend so much time in often frigid weather . . . waiting endless hours for an elusive prey. I began to dislike this sport that took Chris away for so many hours on weekends. Then, one day, Chris convinced me to pick up a bow; and my life was changed forever! I discovered that shooting a bow is empowering; and sitting in a treestand is humbling. I literally wept at the beauty and peace surrounding me on my first hunt. Even though I didn't see a deer that day, it didn't matter. Hunting had given me a new appreciation for my husband, the serenity in nature, and God's creatures.

Always wear a Safety Harness in a Treestand

One of my scariest experiences hunting was on my first walk, ~ 1 mile, alone in the dark. First, I panicked since I could barely find the base of my stand. Next, I empathized with our military and the terror they must feel on a mission in unfamiliar territory. Finally, still shaking, I climbed to the top of the stand and grabbed the shooting rail for support to hang my bow. I forgot that this rail moves! I nearly fell out of the stand, but my safety harness caught me. Had I not been wearing my harness, you might not be reading this.

Never Place Anything Dangerous Below the Stand

I was alone when I fell from my stand while taking the photo of my Bible herein. It was very funny, only because I was wearing a harness. I was about to climb my ladder stand when I noticed thorns growing along one side. I went to reach for the other side until I saw

"IT" ~ my Alien Caterpillar. It had bulging orange eyes, protruding green lips, and I am sure it was smiling at me. I also thought I heard a bear crack a limb nearby since our trail

camera photographed several just a few yards away; and I definitely heard the terrifying thrum of bees. In my solemn chaos, I grabbed the side with the thorns, screamed, let go, and fell backwards by a whopping 4' drop. Although a short distance, my harness saved me from being impaled by the limb cutters I had left beneath me. I recited Habakkuk 3:19 as I made my second ascent. I laughed as I bled while taking that photo.

Get Organized

Since I wear make-up hunting, in anticipation of getting a deer and photo, it takes me longer to get ready in the morning. It is unfair to ask others to wait on you; and the sun certainly won't. Today, I make a list and pack essentials the evening prior. We have socks or slings ready for rifles or bows. I pack my safety harness vest pockets with a rangefinder, Glock, broadheads, bullets, fully charged phone (ringer off), spare safety harness clip, and Sweet Tarts. A radio, water, snack, gloves, and blaze orange hat are perhaps the most important backpack items in case of an emergency in a remote area.

Above All – Have Faith – and Trust in God's Plan

Chris and I "over-the-moon" happy in this photo, and not just about his trophy buck. We now know that God has perfect timing and a much better plan than ours.

God's Plan for Us

After this manner therefore pray ye:
Our Father which art in heaven, Hallowed be thy name. Thy kingdom come.
Thy will be done in earth, as it is in heaven
~ Matthew 6:9-10 KJV

One morning on my way to work, I thought I had an epiphany. I was thinking about God's plan, and for some reason, the "Lord's prayer" came to me. I halted and was stunned by the possible meaning of "thy will be done". I had always thought that this prayer meant that we should behave in the same manner here on Earth as we would in Heaven. I reconsidered the word "thy". Perhaps the prayer I had been reciting nearly every day since my childhood was trying to tell me something; specifically, that we are to work according to God's will, rather than our will. After researching this scripture in several versions of the Bible, here is what I found:

In this manner, therefore, pray:
Our Father in heaven, Hallowed be Your name. Your kingdom come.
Your will be done
~ Matthew 6:9-10 NKJV and NIV

So when you pray, you should pray like this: Our Father in heaven, may your name always be kept holy. May your kingdom come and
what you want be done
~ Matthew 6:9-10 NKJV

While the words finally have concrete meaning to me, I still have much to learn. God's will is the way to happiness. When we finally trusted; and let go, and let God, we found peace in our souls. I pray the same for you.

If God is for us, then who can be against us?
~ Romans 8:31 NIV

Stocking the Pantry

Delicious meals start with great ingredients. A few of my favorite pantry items follow. See Resources, page 266, for more info on specialty items.

Salt & Pepper – Choose finely ground sea salts for even distribution in baked goods and breads. Use coarse crystals, flakes, and grey sea salts for cooking or finishing. Try Le Saunier de Camargue Fleur de Sel and Maldon® Sea Salt. For peppercorns, spicy black Tellicherry are my go-to. Also try green, Szechuan, white, pink, and blends.

Fresh First – Use fresh citrus juice, fruit, vegetables, herbs, and alliums (garlic, leeks, shallots, chives), rather than canned, tubed, or bottled items whenever possible. Look for parsley, tarragon, cilantro, dill, basil, thyme, rosemary, etc. in the produce aisle.

Exceptions to the Rule – A few exceptional dried herbs can often infuse dishes with even greater intensity than fresh aromatics. My favorites include: fennel pollen, fennel seeds, lemon pepper blends, dried pepper flakes, Vadouvan curry, smoked paprika, and Moroccan rubs. Fennel seed is that savory essence in a superb sausage, and pollen has an intense sweetness making it fantastic in anything from main courses to desserts.

Cardamom, Cocoa & Baking –
Transform baked *goods* into *greats* with phenomenal spices, pure vanilla, and quality chocolates. Grate whole nutmeg with a Microplane, seek out Saigon cinnamon and Indian ginger, and make your kitchen smell like heaven with fresh cardamom. Toast the pastel green pods in a dry skillet for 4 min on med-high heat. Crack the shells, remove the seeds, and crush

them with a mortal and pestle. Ready to use cardamom is also available as an extract, preground powder, or as French Essential Oil Crystals (try Florisens). For vanilla, use McCormick's Pure, or, try Nielsen Massey's line of Origin Extracts, Beans, and Pastes. For chocolate, seek out natural cocoa (by Scharffen Berger), and baking squares or chips (by Ghirardelli). For maple, use pure syrup; or try India Tree's Maple Sugar.

Oils & Vinegars – For oils, I primarily use olive for sautéing, butter for browning, peanut for stir-frying, and sesames for flavor. In baking, use unsalted butter for most, coconut oil as shortening, and canola when oil is called for. For salads, experiment with extra virgin olive oils to find your favorite. When it comes to vinegar, like notable wines, you can't go wrong with French, Italian, and Spanish varietals. Look for some of the white wine, red wine, champagne, and sherry labels below at your local gourmet shops. Ariston® offers a particularly sweet and luscious balsamic. Eden's salty Ume Plum is unlike anything else. Also try tarragon infused, organic ciders, and malt vinegars.

Asian Sauces, Wines, and Vinegars – Asian ingredients need not be limited to ethnic dishes. Soy or shoyu sauce is a tasty alternative to salt. White rice vinegars add tartness to bean or grain salads, and tang to sushi. When blended with salt, sugar, and dry Sake or sweet Mirin (white rice wines), it is labeled as seasoned rice vinegar. Use Chinese black rice vinegar or aged rice wines (Shaoxing or Shao Hsing) in stir-fries or anywhere that Sherry is called for. While countless bottled stir-fry sauces are available, you can easily create authentic dishes by blending a few base ingredients with rice wines and vinegars. I keep our fridge stocked with hoisin, chili bean, and chili garlic sauces for stir-fry at a moments notice. Try Lee Kum Kee's versatile line-up of sauces.

Sea Vegetables and Miso – Eden Foods is a fantastic source for an extensive range of super healthy sea vegetables. I keep kombu, wakame, arame, hiziki, nori, wasabi roasted nori, wakame on hand for weekly use. They stay fresh indefinitely in airtight containers; and a little goes a long way. This is also true for refrigerated miso paste.

Coconut Water – Coconut water is conveniently available in cans, bottles, cartons, or, inside coconuts. This natural nectar is incredibly delicious and can be extracted from the mature (brown) fruit on a cutting board in your kitchen, rather than outside with garage tools. I use a metal BBQ skewer and chef's knife to open the drupe. A dehusked coconut has a visible face comprised of 3 pores: 2 eyes (closer together), and a mouth (further away). First, pierce the mouth, which is the softest hole, with the skewer. Rotate it to enlarge this hole. Next, carefully pierce 1 or 2 more holes to create air vents. If these don't pierce readily by pushing and rotating the skewer, hold the coconut steady on the board and tap the top edge of your skewer with a mortar pestle. Pour the clear liquid into a bowl, over a sieve, to filter any fibrous husk. Now, extract the raw meat from the shell. Hold the coconut with one hand with the equator facing you. This is the ridge that runs around the circumference of the shell (between the eyes and opposite end). Tap this seam firmly with the BACK (blunt) side of a knife or cleaver. Rotate and tap until the shell splits open. This may happen after 2 taps; or require a few minutes of tapping. When a crack is visible, pry the shell in half with the skewer. Bake the halves at 350 °F for 20 min to help release the flesh. Wedge the skewer between the shell and meat to pop it out. Cautiously peel the brown skin with a vegetable peeler. Grate the meat by hand or with a food processor.

Kalamatas & Other Drupes – Drupes, also known as stone fruits, typically consist of a fibrous skin, fleshy meat, and a shell containing its seed. My darling drupes are coffee beans and olives. Black olives result when greens are fully ripened. Seek out auburn Greek Kalamatas and black French Niçoise. These rich flavorful varieties differ significantly from canned black olives, which are artificially ripened with ferrous sulfate.

Red Hot Chili Peppers – You can count on Spanish Chiles de Arbol (green stems attached and often sold as wreaths) or Chinese Tien Tsin chilies to intensify marinades, Kung Pao, and curries. For chilies, salsas, and salads, try Chipotle Peppers in Spicy Adobo Sauce by La Preferida®. These smoked jalapeños are exceptionally flavorful.

Molcajetes – Volcanic molcajetes (mortar) and tejoletes (pestle) must be seasoned (smoothed) to remove small lava chips before using. It is best to do this outside. Grind white rice into a powder. Repeat with new rice until the powder is white (free of grey).

Whole Grains, Legumes & Wheatgrass – When purchasing whole grains in bulk (rather than pre-packaged), inspect a bagful for weevils. This tiny black pest is common in old white flour and can cause an infestation. For legumes, always inspect handfuls for small

pebbles or stones before cooking. While wheatgrass is sometimes sold at Whole Foods Markets, it is difficult to find in small towns. Luckily, it is easy to sprout, and then grow. Try a Ball® jar with a strainer lid to sprout; and look for wheatgrass kits with Azomite.

Resources

Our Church

- Auburn Baptist Church, 3840 Riner Rd., Riner, VA, (540) 382-8824

Local Whole Grains and Specialty Food Items

- Eats Natural Foods: 708 N Main St., Blacksburg, VA, 540-552-2279
- Annie Kay's Whole Foods: 1531 S Main St., Blacksburg, VA, 540-552-6870
- Gourmet Pantry: 401 S. Main St., Blacksburg, VA, 540-951-1995
- Oasis World Market: 1411 S Main St. Blacksburg, VA, (540) 953-3950
- Provisions Gourmet: 4235 Electric Rd., Roanoke, VA, 540-857-5888
- Harvest Moon Food Store: 227 N. Locust St., Floyd, VA, 540-745-4366

National Whole Grains and Flour

- Bob's Red Mill: http://www.bobsredmill.com
- Vitacost: http://www.vitacost.com
- King Arthur Flour: http://www.kingarthurflour.com
- Arrowhead Mills: http://www.arrowheadmills.com

Jalapeño & Chipotle Flakes, Fennel Pollen, Lemon Pepper, and Vadouvan

- Victoria Gourmet: http://www.vgourmet.com
- My Spice Sage: http://www.myspicesage.com
- Dean & DeLuca: http://www.deandeluca.com

Lentils le Puy (AOP / AOC), French Sea Salts, and Vinegars

- The Frenchy Bee: http://www.thefrenchybee.com
- Ariston: http://www.aristonoliveoil.com
- Amazon: http://www.amazon.com

Black Turtle, Flageolet, Heirloom, and Good Mother Stallard Beans

- Purcell Mountain Farms: http://www.purcellmountainfarms.com
- Mohr-Frey Ranches: http://www.mohrfry.com
- Bob's Red Mill: http://www.bobsredmill.com

Miso Pastes and Sea Vegetables

- Local: Eats, Annie Kay's, Harvest Moon, and Oasis
- South River Miso Company: http://www.southrivermiso.com
- Eden Foods: http://www.edenfoods.com

Cooking Equipment, Pastry Bag Holders, Spice Bags, and Supplies

- Gourmet Pantry: Blacksburg, VA, http://www.gourmetpantryonline.com
- Provisions Gourmet: Roanoke, VA, http://www.provisionsrsvp.com
- Williams-Sonoma: http://www.williams-sonoma.com
- Sur La Table: http://www.surlatable.com
- Napa Style: http://www.napastyle.com
- Amazon: http://www.amazon.com

Grain Mills, Juicers, and Wheatgrass

- http://www.pleasanthillgrain.com
- https://originalslowjuicer.com
- http://www.wheatgrasskits.com

Local Hunting Supplies and Archery

- Matt Hagan Outdoors: 6125 Warren Newcome Dr., Radford, VA, (540) 838-2282
  - See Chris Ramrattan for Archery and Firearm Expertise
- Whitetail Outfitters: 3086 Riner Rd., Christiansburg, VA, (540) 381-9790

Taxidermists

- Chris Ramrattan, Riner, VA, 540-320-8705
- Anthony Graves, Hunter's Burden, Elliston, VA, 540-871-4839
- Inquire with your local hunting shop for resources

Deer Processing in VA and Abroad

- Hunters for the Hungry: http://www.h4hungry.org/process.htm
- This Virginia Hunters Who Care website features a list of meat processors that participate in the Hunters for the Hungry program. Search for programs like this in your state to find local resources.

Local Deer Processing

- Montgomery County:
  - Hunter's Burden, Elliston, VA, 540-871-4839
  - Harvey's Meat Processing, Radford, VA, 540-731-3093
  - Taylor's Meat Cutting, Christiansburg, VA, 540-382-1323
- Floyd County: Willis Village Mart, Willis, VA, 540-789-7241
- Giles County: Smith Valley Meats, Rich Creek, VA, 540-726-3992
- Roanoke County: Overstreet Food, Inc., Roanoke, VA, 540-342-3860

Professional Photography Local and Abroad

- Lucky Shot Photography: http://luckyshotphotography.zenfolio.com
- Photography by Drena: http://drenasphotography.com
- PFS Photo: http://www.pfsphoto.com

French Cooking Classes and Macarons

- http://lacuisineparis.com and http://www.laduree.com/en_int/

Marketing Services

- Salvo Media, LLC: www.Salvo.me contact Danny Salvaterra at: dan@salvo.me

Guided Trips for Saskatchewan Fish, Whitetail Deer, and Black Bear

- Poplar Point: http://www.poplarpointresort.com/index.php, 306-469-4987 contact Victor and Sally Dorval at: poplarpointresort@hotmail.com

Father, Son, & Daughter-in-Law
in Saskatchewan with Horns in Hand & Meat in Cooler

References and Credits

References

Websites

- http://www.mayoclinic.com/health/wild-game/MYO1079
- http://www.cancer.org
- http://wholegrainscouncil.org

Books that I Love and Highly Recommend

- Allen, Phil, and K.K. Fowlkes and Chuck Juhn; Living Whole Foods, Inc. *Wheatgrass, Sprouts, Microgreens, and the Living Food Diet*. Springville, UT: Living Whole Foods, Inc., LM Publications, 2010.

- Backes, Miriam, and The Bob's Red Mill® Family. *Bob's Red Mill® Cookbook, Whole & Healthy Grains for Every Meal of the Day*. Philadelphia, PA: Running Press Book Publishers, 2009.

- Biblica, Inc.™. *The Holy Bible, New International Version® NIV®*. Grand Rapids, MI: Zondervan®, 2011.

- Brown, Simon. *Modern-Day Macrobiotics, Transform Your Diet and Feed Your Mind, Body, and Spirit*. Berkeley, CA: North Atlantic Books, 2007.

- Burkitt, MD Denis P. *Don't Forget Fibre in your Diet*. London, Harper Collins, 1980.

- Child, Julia, Louisette Bertholle, Simone Beck, and Sidonie Coryn. *Mastering the Art of French Cooking: Volume One*. New York: Alfred A. Knopf, 40th Anniversary ed., 2000.

- Ettinger, John, and The Bob's Red Mill® Family. *Bob's Red Mill® Baking Book*. Philadelphia, PA: Running Press Book Publishers, 2006.

- Keller, Thomas, with Jeffrey Cerciello, Susie Heller, and Michael Ruhlman. *Bouchon*. New York: Artisan, 2004.

- Lucado, Max, General Editor. *Holy Bible, New Century Version, The Everyday Bible, The Inspirational Study Bible, Life Lessons from The Inspired Word of God*. Dallas, TX: Word Publishing, 1995.

- Lewis, C.S. *The Screwtape Letters*. New York: Harper Collins Publishers, 1940 / 1996.

- Lewis, C.S. *The Problem of Pain*. New York: Harper Collins Publishers, 1940 / 1996.
- Mossy Oak®. *The Holy Bible, Authorized King James Version, Great Outdoors Bible*. Nashville: Thomas Nelson, Inc., 2001.
- Muir, Jenni. *A Cook's Guide to Grains: delicious recipes, culinary advice and nutritional facts*. Heron Quays, London: Conran, Octopus Limited, 2008.
- Nee, Watchman. *New Believer's Series*. Anaheim, CA: Living Stream Ministry, Slipcase edition, 1997.
- Porter, Jessica. *The Hip Chick's guide to Macrobiotics, a Philosophy for Achieving a Radiant Mind and Fabulous Body*. New York: Avery, A Member of Penguin Group (USA), Inc., 2004.
- Reinhart, Peter. *Whole Grain Breads: New Techniques, Extraordinary Flavor*. Berkeley / Toronto: Ten Speed Press, 2011.
- King Arthur Flour®, Ruopp, Wendy. *King Arthur Flour® Whole Grain Baking, Delicious Recipes Using Nutritious Whole Grains*. Woodstock, VT: The Countryman Press, 2006.
- Sass, Lorna. *Whole Grains Every Day, Every Way*. New York: Crown Publishing Group, Clarkson Potter/Publishers, 2006.
- Schmidt, Cary. *done: What most religions don't tell you about the Bible*. Lancaster, CA: Striving Together Publications, 2005.
- Thomas Nelson Inc. *The Holy Bible, New King James Version®*. Nashville: Thomas Nelson, Inc., 1982.
- Wigmore, Ann. *The Wheatgrass Book*. New York: Avery, A Member of Penguin Group (USA), Inc., 1985.
- Wood, Rebecca. *The Splendid Grain*. New York: William Morrow and Company, HarperCollins Publishers 1998.

Credits

Afterward

I began writing this book after a sad time in my life, to focus on all things positive and move beyond despair. What started as a constructive way to fulfill an old dream, ended with a miracle. Writing this book required me to record the recipes for dishes we love. More importantly, it caused me to research the nutritional reasons for my recovered health, and to appreciate the spiritual ones. I learned more about the Bible, life, and cooking than I could have imagined, and have immensely enjoyed this endeavor.

My parents taught me that if I worked hard enough, anything would be possible. For the most part, they were correct. First, I married my soul mate and best friend. Next, I embarked on an amazing professional career in nanotechnology. Then, I got to relive my childhood with Chris outdoors through hunting. Finally, I found God, and accepted His grace. The latter is what I am most thankful for; yet required the least amount of work. Similarly, while hard work result has resulted in nice kitchen things for me, God's grace is free; and once you know Him, it cannot be taken from you.

The main thing I learned on this journey is that accepting God's grace and trusting in God's plan are two very different things. For me, believing in God has always been easy. I believe that the natural beauty that surrounds us, and the tears of joy that these creations evoke, cannot be anything but divine. Though, giving up control and trusting in God's plan, is daunting for a type-A from the instant gratification generation. For me, this meant doing things on God's time and not forcing things. Once I realized that time belongs to God, and not me, my life changed forever. I'll leave the details to your imagination, and perhaps detail them in another book. For now, I pray that you have the will power to follow your heart, rather than your plan. To quote my Pastor, "Don't give up on your dreams, and don't give up on God. He won't give up on you. HE WANTS TO SURPRISE YOU". My greatest hope for this book is that something here makes you smile - whether it be an idea, story, or health benefit from one of the recipes. Smiles are the light bulbs of our souls. Smile, and you feel energized, as if you consumed a fresh glass of sunshine powered orange juice. Writing this book made me smile every day.

While writing the book made me smile, the composition was frustrating at times. A novelist told me that writing the book was the easy part. I get that now. For a cookbook, additional logistics include recipe testing, methodical consistency, photography, nutritional facts, an index, sketches, copyright issues, and of course, publishing. In today's digital world, finding a publisher willing to risk printing hard copies was not possible. Once I went back to the original intent, *to focus on the positive*, rather than personal deadlines or others' opinions, it was again a joy rather than a job.

When I started writing this book, I thought it would be easy since I had thousands of photographs of our favorite meals on reserve. My plan was to cook, document, retest, and pair recipes with existing images. None of these photographs were of use. They did not resemble any photos in books I paid money for. I added photography to my list of new endeavors. Chris took me to see, *Fast and the Furious 6*. I loved it, of course, but walked out more determined than ever. I could not fathom how they could capture racecars in mid-air; yet I could not get one decent photo of food, sitting there, perhaps laughing at me. Input from professionals, Photography by Drena (my cousin in TX), Tammy at Lucky Shot, and PFS Photo, was a Godsend. I learned through trial and error (a lot), and began to have fun (more than a lot), with every small success.

Try something new today and share your findings with friends tomorrow. I could not understand my husband's obsession with hunting years ago until I tried it. Feasting on a great meal, hunting on a crisp Fall morning, and accepting God's will for your life are good examples of things that must be experienced before dismissing.

Every single morning, I literally jump out of bed between 4 and 6 AM. I can't wait to give our cat his favorite treat, make fresh juice, bring coffee to Chris, and harass him with the latest plans. I return to my coffee chair, say thank you to God, and plan the best day possible. Everyday is a gift. I say thank you to everyone, and for everything I can think of. I thank Jesus for my joy and trust God with my challenges. He will never give you more than you can handle. Each and every day, hug your spouse, e-mail your friends, dance with your cat to a country song, pray for everyone you know on a 5k-prayer run, and try a new recipe from *Hunt & Gather*. Eat every meal, with a smile, as though it may be your last supper.

Thanks be to God, Family & Friends

Thank You God, our Father, for blessing us with free will to enjoy Your Heavenly land. Thank you especially for wild game, bountiful grains, and loved ones to share it all with.

Thank you to: my husband and best friend, Chris, for your love, support, patience, and wit, reflected in your recurring question, "Will we be cooking by flash photography tonight." For teaching me to hunt, believe, share, and be a kid again. To our miracles, Barlow, Alexandra, and Tristan Hunter, for our present, past, and future. To Mom and Dad, Rosemary and Joseph Hoyt, for your selfless love, sacrifices, work ethic, humor, and teaching me everything. To my kindhearted brother Joey, for being you. To my amazing in-laws, Kathy and Captain Lou Lalli, for your love, editing, and 7mm Weatherby Magnum. To Laurel, Todd, Tyler, Matthew, and Caitlin Bernard for making family fun, and helping bake and eat hundreds of cookies. To Aunt Pet and Uncle John Plucenik for your lifelong prayers and the Independent NEPA feature. To Dr. Richard Claus for teaching me to prioritize by impact. To Dick and Annie Krull for teaching us to let go.

Thank you to: my dearest friends, taste testers, and editors. To Dr. Susan Willis who encouraged this cookbook with giddy enthusiasm. To Chris and Jess Ramrattan, Kim and Bryan Rodichok, Erik and Laura Robinson, Lee Winkle, Sarah McPeak, Lee Johnson, Dr. Maggie Bump, Dave Rash, Mary Kate Gaines, Dr. Katie Amelink, CPT Keith and Andrea Hill, Shannon Keough, Kelly Dorish-Bladek, Carol and Kimberly Staub, and everyone at NanoSonic. To Grandmas Elizabeth, Ruth, and Annie, and Grandpa Hoyt and Grandpa Guillory. To MSGT Michael and Drena Spatharos, SGTE5 Dave Sisson, and SSGT Wesley

Hodges for your support and serving our Country. To Danny Salvaterra, Al and Ellen Fletcher, Dr. James Weston, Pastor Shake Smith, and our Auburn Baptist Church family, for your faith. To Kevin Finley and Megan Carroll at Hillcrest Media, Andrew Connors at the Creekmore Law Firm, and Brad McConnell P.C.

Index

Giving Back - Hunt for JOY, L.L.C.

A portion of the profits from this book will be donated to charity from Hunt for JOY

www.huntforjoy.com

- <u>Mission</u> - Hunt for JOY is a company dedicated to nourishing the spiritually and physically hungry.

- <u>Promise</u> – More than 50% of the profits from this book will be donated to Auburn Baptist Church, the Wounded Warrior Project™, Project Healing Waters Fly Fishing, Inc.™, and more. Contact us at jen@huntforjoy.com for bulk discounts and donations to your tax exempt cause.

- <u>Method</u> – Dr. Jennifer Lalli's cookbooks validate the powers of whole grains, lean meat, and prayer. With a Ph.D. in polymer chemistry, she used her laboratory and literature review expertise to develop delicious whole grain recipes for every day enjoyment. Along the way, she took up hunting under her husband's tutelage. On their hunt for deer, they found God. Venison has changed their lives forever. Through these recipes, Jennifer healed herself physically and spiritually. *Hunt & Gather* is the first in a series of cookbooks that celebrate the outdoors and God's bountiful gifts.

Jennifer Hoyt Lalli is a native of Swoyersville, PA. She received her Ph.D. in Polymer Chemistry from Virginia Tech, and is the EV President of NanoSonic, Inc., a company scaling nanotechnology in Giles County, VA. After years of research in the field and kitchen, she formed Hunt for JOY, L.L.C. to publish her most significant findings to date - that prayer and chemistry through nutrition - are capable of healing. She currently resides in Blacksburg, VA with her husband, Chris, and two children, Tristan Hunter and Milla Fisher. Together, they hunt, gather, and celebrate the miracle of life.

Hunt for JOY

www.huntforjoy.com

CPSIA information can be obtained
at www.ICGtesting.com
Printed in the USA
BVHW021159110122
625996BV00018B/457